COVERS

SCAN THE SPOTIFY CODES TO PLAY EVERY ALBUM INSTANTLY!

1.

Click the search bar in your **spotify** app.
Then tip the camera icon at the top right.

2.

Scan the printed **spotify**
code on the calendar page.

3.

Enjoy the music!

“I’m a big collector of vinyl – I have a record room in my house – and I’ve always had a huge soundtrack album collection. So what I do, as I’m writing a movie, is go through all those songs, trying to find good songs for fights, or good pieces of music to layer into the film.”

Quentin Tarantino

Cinema for the Ears

Even before you've heard a single note, a simple first glance at the artwork reveals much of the magic inherent in a soundtrack away from the cinema screen. The wide range of styles is just as eclectic as the musical genres behind the artwork: movie poster motifs and illustrations, movie stills and graphic design, comics and pop art, watercolours and collages; sometimes it's the details, then it's back to panoramas and crowd scenes.

Let's thumb through the first few days of the new year. Look, here's the wonderful Jessica getting onto her vespa to the music of Mario Nascimbene, followed by The Mercenary firing his pistol to the splendid musical accompaniment from the masterful Ennio Morricone, and then there's Mad Max and Tina Turner telling us that We Don't Need Another Hero.

Three pages that portray a whole universe, and we're only just getting started. Flick through each day to see soundtracks from the film industry's past, featuring Henry Mancini, John Barry, Vince Guaraldi, Isaac Hayes, Michel Polnareff, and Sid Ramin, all elaborately designed by celebrated artists such as Saul Bass, Bob Peak, and Frank Frazetta.

Soundtracks on vinyl is a fascinating marrying together of film posters with a visit to the movies; it's adventure in miniature, cinematic pleasure at 33 RPM. The visuals act as an emotional link between cinema seat and headphones, a spot in the stalls and the lounge armchair at home. Get your soundtrack ticket punched and be ready for lights, camera, action! Welcome to new year packed full of vinyl art. Every day covers a new film, a new world, its own planet.

Cinema for the Ears: The Art of Soundtrack Covers.

Ingo Scheel
Record Collector, Music and Movie Journalist
Hamburg, January 2021

JAZZ MUSEUM HAMBURG
Side Sections
Pop and others
10812

JESSICA • UNITED ARTISTS • STEREO • UAS 5096

MOTION PICTURE SOUND TRACK ALBUM

JEAN NEGULESCO'S

Jessica

MAURICE CHEVALIER
•
ANGIE DICKINSON
•
NOEL-NOEL

† Jan 1st, 1972 as Maurice Auguste Chevalier in Paris, France

Jessica
Maurice Chevalier
United Artists Records, 1962
Jean Negulesco (Director)

01

JAN

The Mercenary
Ennio Morricone
United Artists Records, 1969
Sergio Corbucci (Director)

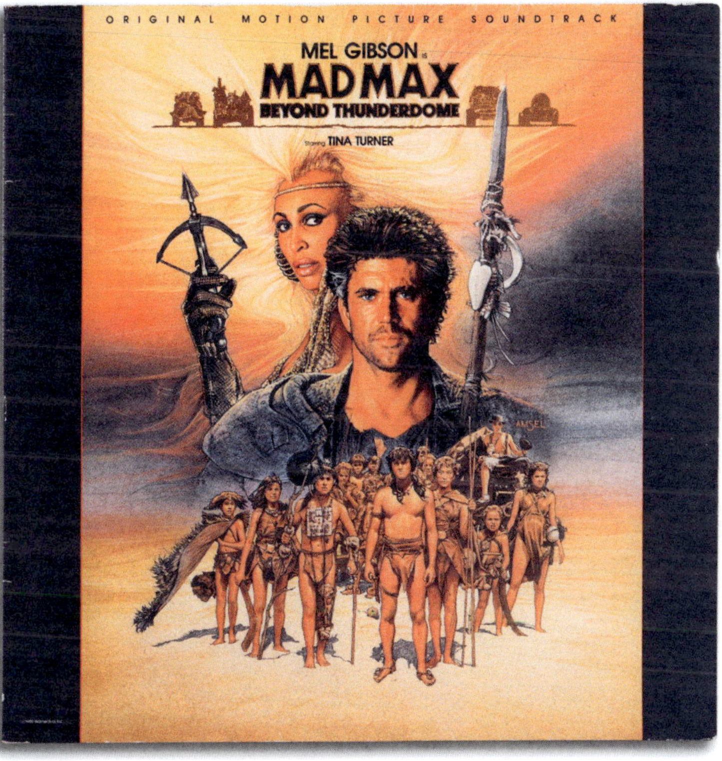

* Jan 3rd, 1956 as Mel Gibson in Peekskill, New York, USA

Mad Max Beyond Thunderdome
Maurice Jarre
Capitol Records, 1985
George Miller & George Ogilvie (Director)
Richard Amsel (Design)

03

JAN

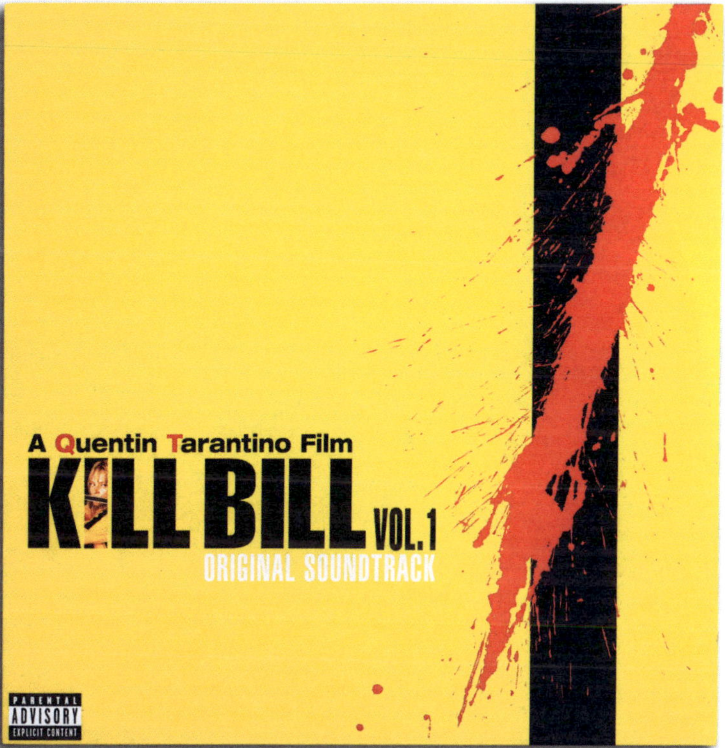

Kill Bill Vol.1
A Band Apart Records, 2003
Quentin Tarantino (Director)
Alon Amir, Marcus Almaraz (Design)

04

JAN

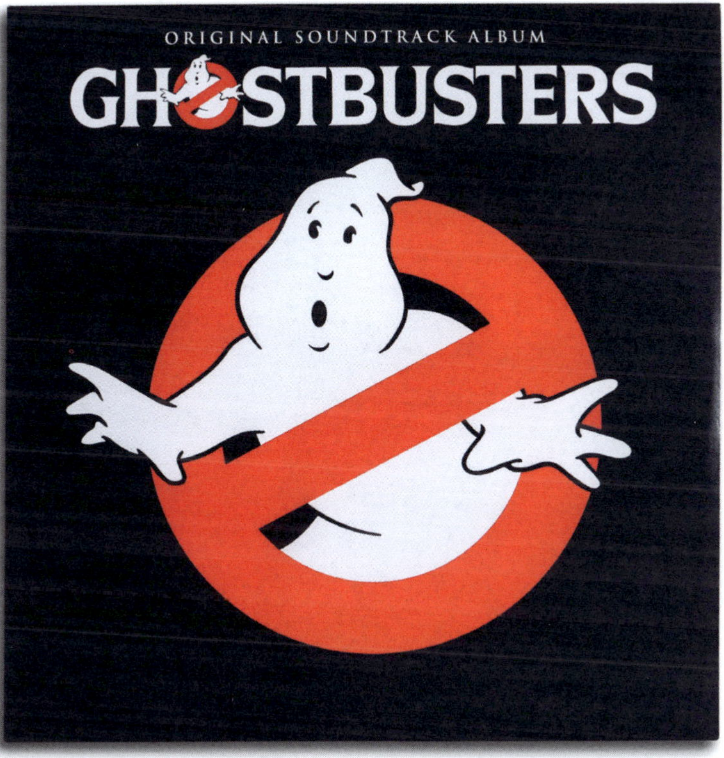

Ghostbusters
Various Artists
Arista Records, 1984
Ivan Reitman (Director)

05

JAN

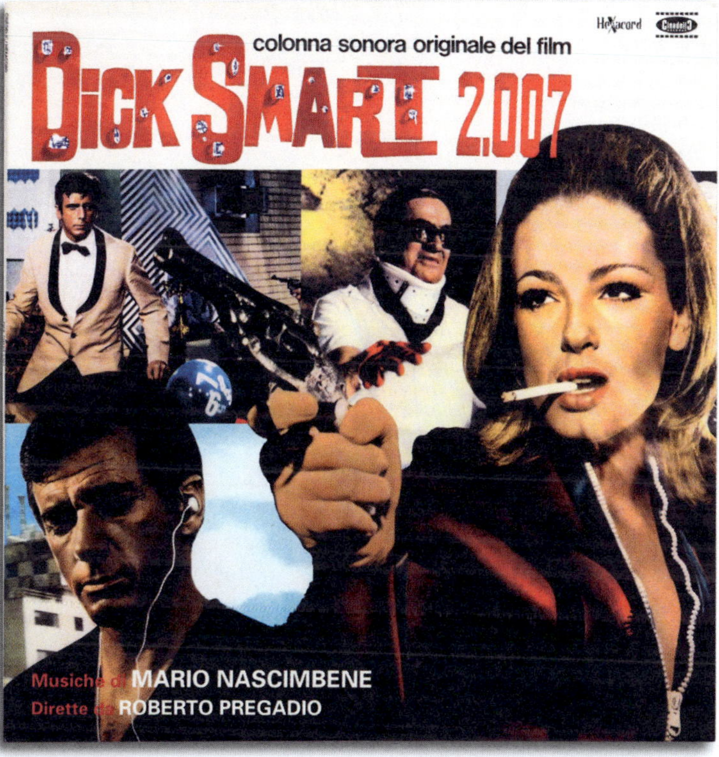

† Jan 6th, 2002 as Mario Nascimbene in Rome, Italia

Dick Smart 2.007
Mario Nascimbene
Cinedelic Records, 1967
Roberto Pregadio (Director)
Marco D'Ubaldo (Design)

Cool Hand Luke
Lalo Schifrin
Dot Records, 1967
Stuart Rosenberg (Director)

07

JAN

* Jan 8th, 1947 as David Robert Jones in London, UK

Labyrinth
Various Artists
EMI Records America, 1986
Jim Henson (Director)
Brian Froud (Design)

08

JAN

* Jan 9th, 1941 as Joan Baez in Staten Island, New York City

Sacco & Vanzetti
Ennio Morricone
RCA Victor, 1971
Giuliano Montaldo (Director)
Simeoni (Design)

09

JAN

† Jan 10th, 2016 as David Robert Jones
in New York City, USA

Christiane F. – Wir Kinder Vom Bahnhof Zoo
David Bowie
RCA Victor, 1981
Ulrich Edel (Director)

10

JAN

The Biggest Bundle Of Them All
Riz Ortolani
MGM Records, 1968
Ken Annakin (Director)
Bob Mcginnis (Design)

11 JAN

Veruschka
Ennio Morricone
Dagored, 2014
Franco Rubartelli (Director)

12

JAN

Times Square
Various Artists
RSO, 1980
Robert Stigwood (Director)
Glenn Ross (Design)

13

JAN

RADIOLA
ESTABLISHED 1970

MR-1099
Adventure Series No. 13
Release No. 99

CASABLANCA
Starring
HUMPHREY BOGART, INGRID BERGMAN
and Paul Henreid
Complete as heard on "The Screenguild Players", broadcast on CBS radio, April 26, 1943.
Sponsored by Lady Esther.

† Jan 14th, 1957 as Humphrey DeForest Bogart
in Los Angeles, California, USA

Casablanca
Max Steiner
The Radiola Co., 1979
Michael Curtiz (Director)

14

JAN

Asphalt Cowboy
Various Artists
United Artists Records, 1969
John Schlesinger (Director)

15

JAN

* Jan 16th, 1948 as John Howard Carpenter
in Carthage, New York, USA

The Thing
Ennio Morricone
MCA Records, 1982
John Carpenter (Director)

16

JAN

* Jan 17th, 1952 as Ryuichi Sakamoto in Tokyo, Japan

Merry Christmas
Ryuichi Sakamoto
London Records, 1983
Nagisa Oshima (Director)
Tsuguya Inoue (Design)

17

JAN

Nausicaä Of The Valley Of The Wind
Joe Hisaishi
Studio Ghibli Records, 2018
Hayao Miyazaki (Director)
Hayao Miyazaki (Design)

18 JAN

* Jan 19th, 1946 as Dolly Rebecca Parton
in Sevierville, Tennessee, USA

Rhinestone
Dolly Parton
RCA Records, 1984
Bob Clark (Director)
Tim Bryant (Design)

19

JAN

† Jan 20th, 1993 as Audrey Hepburn
in Tolochenaz, Switzerland

Breakfast At Tiffany's
Henry Mancini
RCA Records, 1986
Blake Edwards (Director)
Howell Conant (Design)

20

JAN

MUSIC FROM AND INSPIRED BY
DALLAS BUYERS CLUB

Dallas Buyers Club
Various Artists
Music On Vinyl, 2014
Jean-Marc Vallée (Director)

NIGHT ON EARTH

Original Soundtrack Recording

a film by JIM JARMUSCH

music by TOM WAITS

original songs by TOM WAITS & KATHLEEN BRENNAN

* Jan 22th, 1953 as Jim Jarmusch
in Cuyahoga Falls, Ohio, USA

Night On Earth
Tom Waits
Island Records, 1991
Jim Jarmusch (Director)

22

JAN

Convoy
Various Artists
Capitol Records, 1978
Sam Peckinpah (Director)

* Jan 24th, 1941 as Neil Leslie Diamond in New York City, USA

The Jazz Singer
Neil Diamond
Capitol Records, 1980
Richard Fleischer (Director)

24

JAN

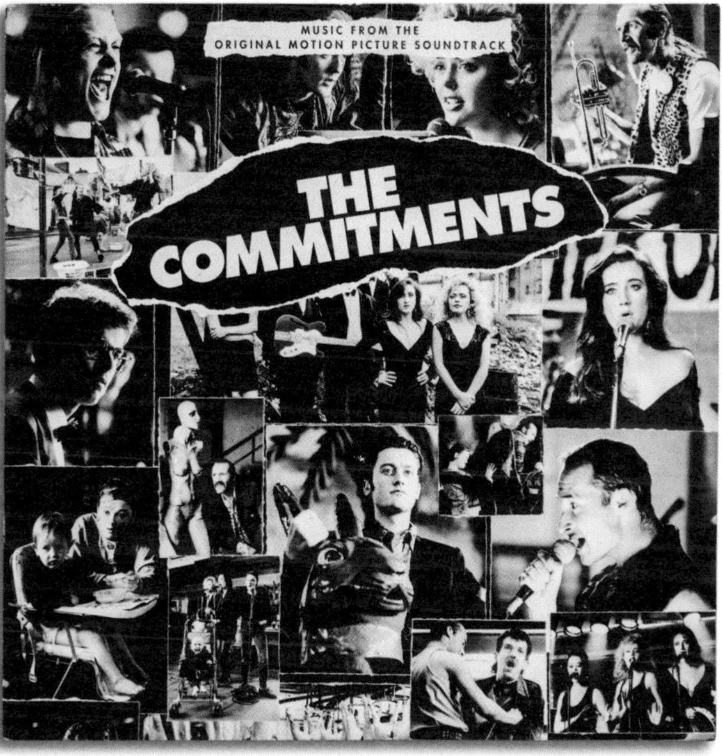

MUSIC FROM THE
ORIGINAL MOTION PICTURE SOUNDTRACK

THE
COMMITMENTS

The Commitments
MCA Records, 1991
David Appleby (Director)
David Appleby (Photo)

25

JAN

† Jan 26th, 2019 as Michel Jean Legrand
in Neuilly-sur-Seine, France

The Thomas Crown Affair
Michael Legrand
Sunset Records, 1968
Norman Jewison (Director)

26

JAN

Miami Vice
Various Artists
MCA Records, 1984
Anthony Yerkovich (Director)
Gusmano Cesaretti (Design)

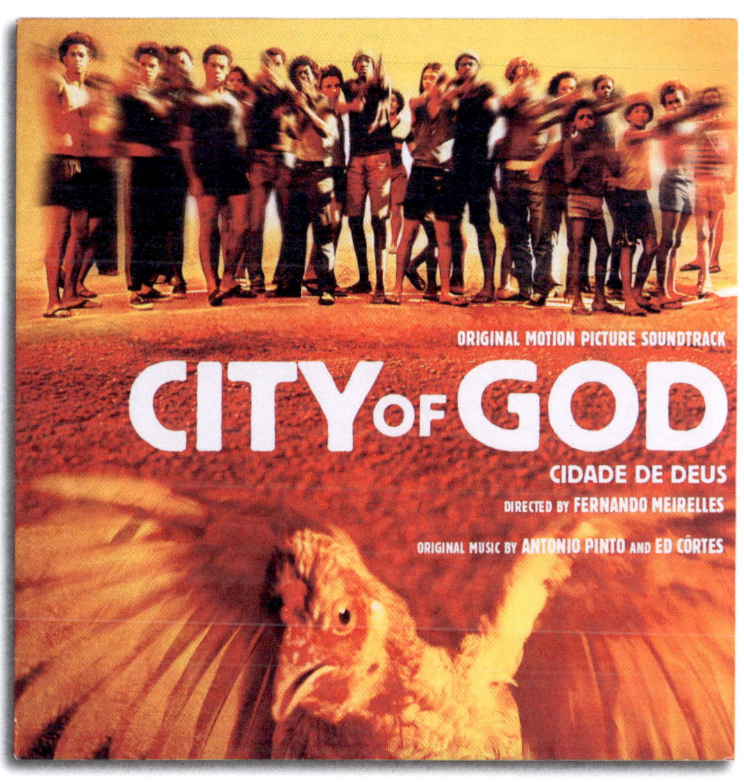

City Of God
Various Artists
Milan, 2003
Fernando Meirelles (Director)

28

JAN

Blade Runner
Vangelis
Full Moon / WEA, 1982
Ridley Scott (Director)

29

JAN

* Jan 30th, 1951 as Philip David Charles "Phil" Collins
in Chiswick, London, UK

Buster
Various Artists
WEA International, 1988
David Green (Director)
Proktor And Storey (Design)

30

JAN

Rock'n'Roll High School
Various Artists
Sire Records, 1979
Allan Arkush (Director)

31

JAN

Over The Edge
Various Artists
Warner Bros. Records, 1979
Jonathan Kaplan (Director)

01

FEB

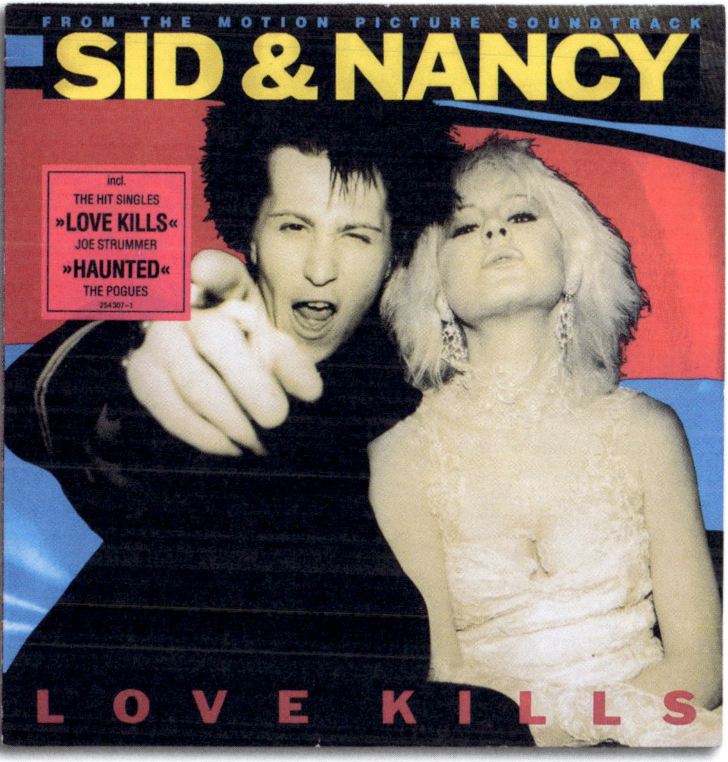

† Feb 2nd, 1979 as Sid Vicious as John Smon Ritchie
in New York, USA

Sid & Nancy
Various Artists
MCA Records, 1986
Alex Cox (Director)

A Hard Days Night
The Beatles
Parlophone, 1964
Richard Lester (Director)

03

FEB

Grand Prix
Maurice Jarre
MGM Records, 1966
John Frankenheimer (Director)

04

FEB

Ian Fleming's 007 Goldfinger
John Barry
United Artists Records, 1964
Guy Hamilton (Director)

05

FEB

ORIGINAL MOTION PICTURE SOUNDTRACK ALBUM

"LADY IN CEMENT"

MUSIC COMPOSED AND CONDUCTED BY
HUGO MONTENEGRO

† Feb 6th, 1981 as Hugo Montenegro
in Palms Springs, California, USA

Lady In Cement
Hugo Montenegro
Harkit Records, 1968
Gordon Douglas (Director)
Tim Noel-Johnson (Design)

06

FEB

Three The Hard Way
The Impressions
Curtom Records, 1974
Gordon Parks Jr. (Director)
Reggie Morrison (Design)

07

FEB

† Feb 8th, 2005 as Jimmy Smith in Phoenix, Arizona, USA

La Métamorphose Des Cloportes
Jimmy Smith
Verve, 1965
Pierre Granier-Deferre (Director)

08

FEB

Full Metal Jacket
Abigail Mead
Warner Bros. Records, 1987
Stanley Kubrick (Director)

Pretty In Pink
Various Artists
A&M Records, 1986
Howard Deutsch (Director)

10

FEB

* Feb 11th, 1936 as Burton Leon Milo Burt Reynolds
in Lansing, Florida, USA

Smokey And The Bandit
Sonny Burke
MCA Records, 1977
Hal Needham (Director)

11 FEB

Solaris
Edward Artemiev
Mirumir Music Publishing, 2013
Andrei Tarkowski (Director)

12

FEB

633 Squadron
Ron Goodwin
E.M.I Records Limited, 1964
Walter Grauman (Director)

13

FEB

American Graffitti
Various Artists
MCA Records, 1973
George Lucas (Director)

14

FEB

† Feb 15th, 1965 as Nat King Cole in Santa Monica, California, USA

Sings His Songs From Cat Ballou
Nat King Cole
Capitol Records, 1965
Elliot Silverstein (Director)

15

FEB

Die Tiefe
John Barry
Casablanca, 1977
Peter Yates (Director)

16

FEB

† Feb 17th as Alfred Newman in Hollywood, L.A, California, USA

The Robe
Alfred Newman
MCA Records, 1953
Henry Koster (Director)

17

FEB

* Feb 18th, 1954 as John Travolta in Englewood, New Jersey, USA

Saturday Night Fever
Various Artists
RSO Records, 1977
John Badham (Director)

18

FEB

* Feb 19th, 1940 as William "Smokey" Robinson, Jr.
in Detroit, Michigan, USA

Big Time
Smokey Robinson
Tamla Motown, 1977
Andrew Georgias (Director)

Big Bad Wolves
Frank Ilfman
Death Waltz Recording Co., 2015
Lance W. Dreesen (Director)
We Buy Your Kids (Design)

20

FEB

The Cotton Club
John Barry
Geffen Records, 1984
Francis Ford Coppola (Director)
Steve Gerdes (Design)

21

FEB

My Fair Lady
Shelly Manne & His Friends
Contemporary Records, 1956
George Cukor (Director)
Robert Guidi (Design)

22

FEB

ORIGINAL SOUNDTRACK OF THE PARAMOUNT MOTION PICTURE

Footloose

KENNY LOGGINS
FOOTLOOSE

SHALAMAR
DANCING IN THE SHEETS

DENIECE WILLIAMS
LET'S HEAR IT FOR THE BOY

MIKE RENO (of "Loverboy")
and ANN WILSON (of "Heart")
ALMOST PARADISE . . .
Love Theme From FOOTLOOSE

BONNIE TYLER
HOLDING OUT FOR A HERO

KENNY LOGGINS
I'M FREE
(HEAVEN HELPS THE MAN)

SAMMY HAGAR
THE GIRL GETS AROUND

KARLA BONOFF
SOMEBODY'S EYES

MOVING PICTURES
NEVER

Footloose
Various Artists
CBS Records, 1983
Herbert Ross (Director)

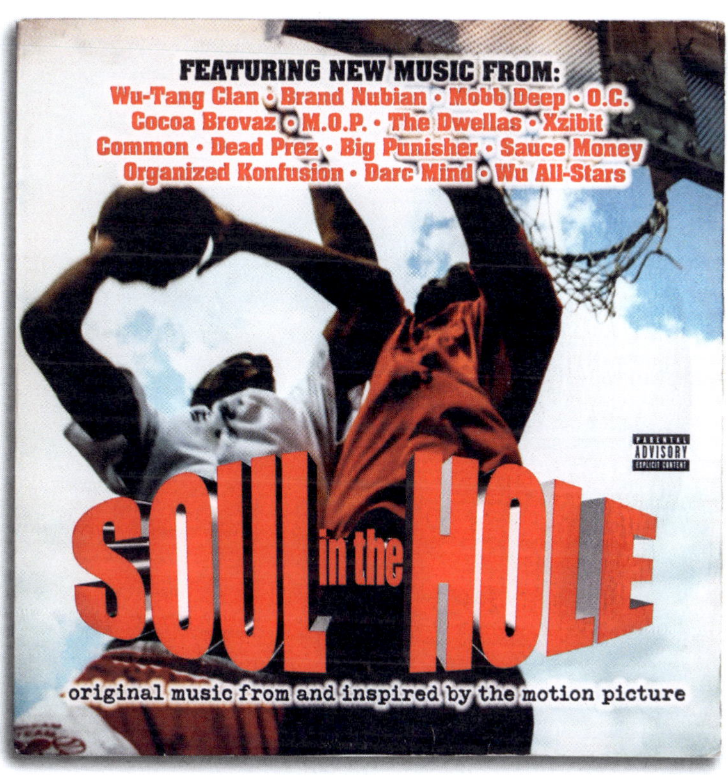

Soul In The Hole
Various Artists
Loud Records, 1997
Danielle Gardner (Director)
Ola Kudu (Design)

24

FEB

Flash Gordon
Queen
EMI Electrola, 1980
Mike Hodges (Director)
Cream (Design)

25

FEB

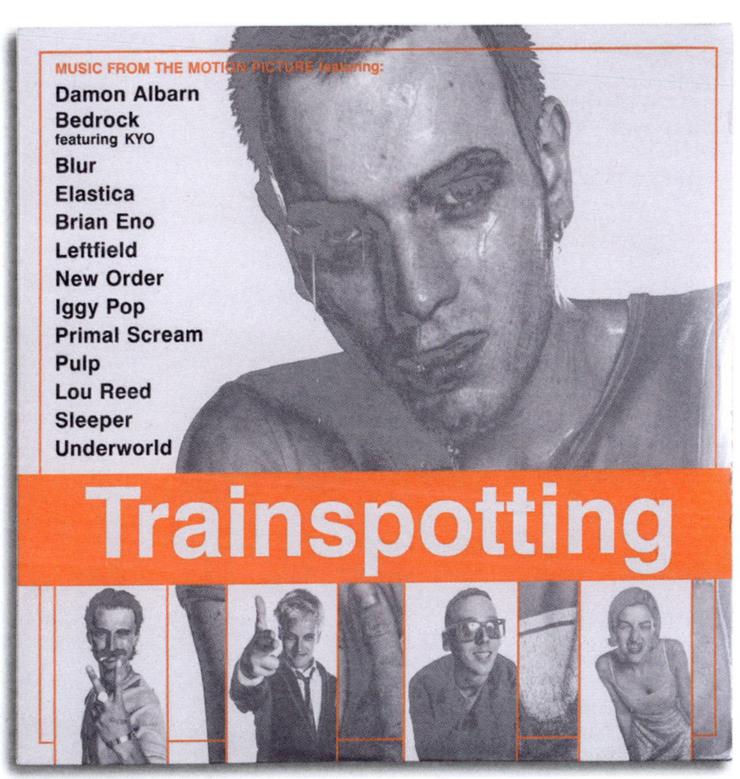

Trainspotting
Various Artists
EMI Electrola, 1996
Danny Boyle (Director)

The Great Waldo Pepper
Henry Mancini
MCA Records, 1975
George Roy Hell (Director)

27

FEB

Rollerball
Andre Previn
United Artists Records, 1975
Norman Jewison (Director)
Bob Peak (Design)

28

FEB

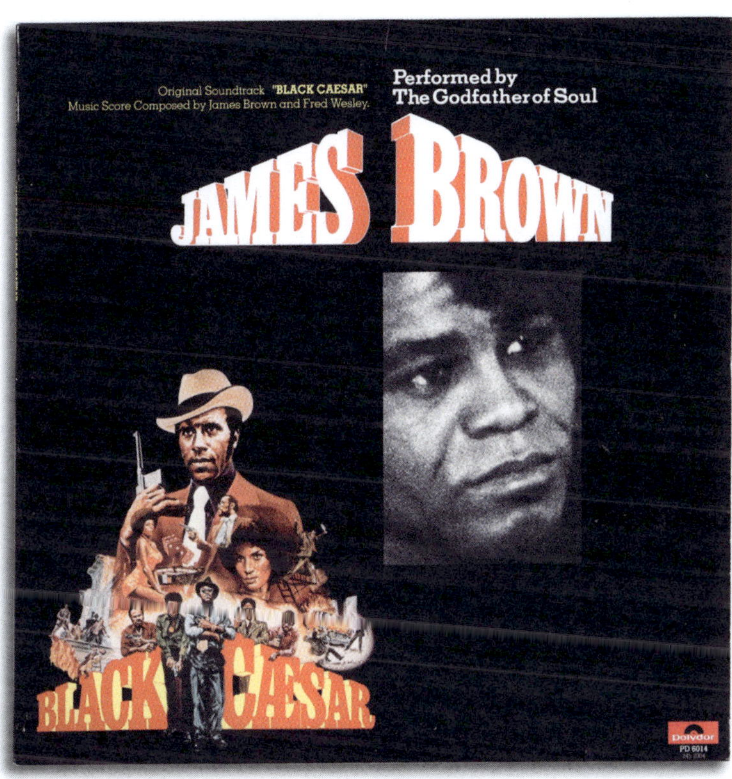

Black Caesar
James Brown
Polydor, 1973
Larry Cohen (Director)

* Mar 1st, 1944 as Roger Harry Daltrey
in Hammersmith, London, UK

The Kids Are Alright
The Who
Polydor Records, 1979
Jeff Stein (Director)
Richard Evans (Design)

01

MAR

Black Fist
Various Artists
Happy Fox Records, 1977
Richard Kaye, Timothy Galfas (Director)
James Graca, Ron Carson (Design)

02

MAR

Gunn... Number One!
Henry Mancini
RCA Victor, 1967
Blake Edwards (Director)

03

MAR

Christine
Various Artists
Motown, 1983
John Carpenter (Director)

04

MAR

Querelle – Ein Pakt mit dem Teufel
Peer Raben
Jupiter Records, 1982
Rainer Werner Fassbinder (Director)
Andy Warhol (Design)

05

MAR

AN ORIGINAL CAST ALBUM
A HIGH FIDELITY RECORDING E3542 ST
RECORDED FROM THE SOUND TRACK
MGM PRESENTS AN ARTHUR FREED PRODUCTION
A DAZZLING MUSICAL IN CINEMASCOPE AND METROCOLOR
M·G·M RECORDS
Silk Stockings

Silk Stockings
André Previn And MGM Studio Orchestra
MGM Records, 1957
Rouben Mamoulian (Director)

06

MAR

† Mar 7th, 1999 as Stanley Kubrick in Childwickbury Manor in London, UK

2001 A Space Odyssey
Various Artists
MGM Records, 1968
Stanley Kubrick (Director)

07

MAR

The Elephant Man
John Morris
Pacific Arts, 1981
David Lynch (Director)
Jerry Takigawa (Design)

08

MAR

The Bridge On The River Kwai
Malcolm Arnold
CBS Records, 1957
David Lean (Director)

09

MAR

The Great Rock 'N' Roll Swindle
Sex Pistols
Virgin, 1980
Julien Temple (Director)
Animation City (Design)

10

MAR

Striptease
Serge Gainsbourg
Striptease, 1963
Jacques Poitrenaud (Director)
Vaissier (Design)

11

MAR

Sol Madrid
Lalo Schifrin
MGM Records, 1968
Brian G. Hutton (Director)
Jack Anesh (Design)

12

MAR

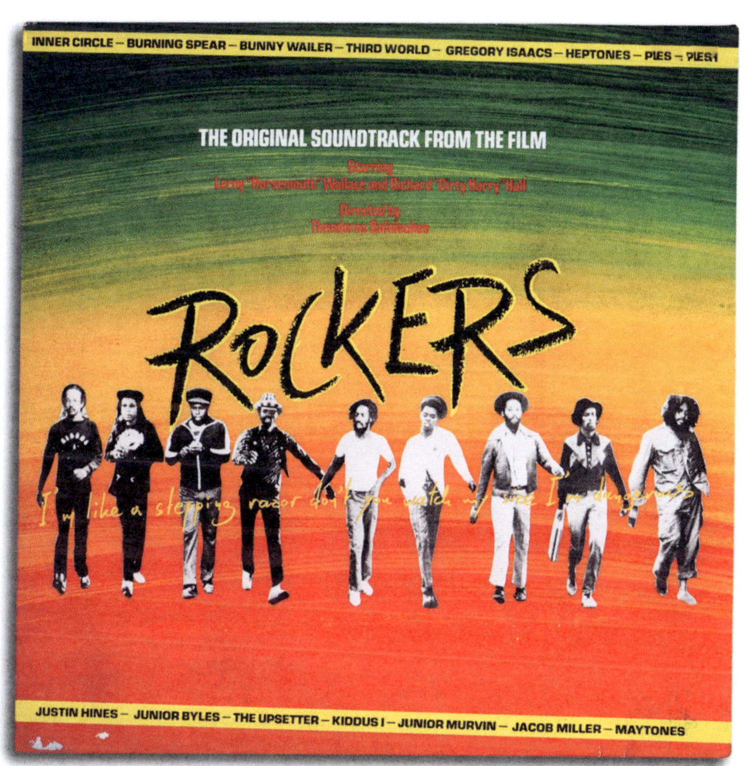

Rockers
Various Artists
Mango Records, 1979
Theodoros Bafaloukos (Director)

13

MAR

* Mar 14th, 1933 as Quincy Delight Jones Jr.
in Chicago, Illinois, USA

They Call Me Mister Tibbs
Quincy Jones
United Artists Records, 1970
Gordon Douglas (Director)
Frank Gauna (Design)

14

MAR

* Mar 15th, 1947 as Ryland Peter Ry Cooder
in Los Angeles, California, USA

Johnny Handsome
Ry Cooder
Warner Bros. Records, 1989
Walter Hill (Director)

ORIGINAL MOTION PICTURE SOUNDTRACK
THE CHAMP
MUSIC BY DAVE GRUSIN
Plus the single "IF YOU REMEMBER ME"

The Champ
Dave Gruisin
MGM Records, 1979
Franco Zeffirelli (Director)

16

MAR

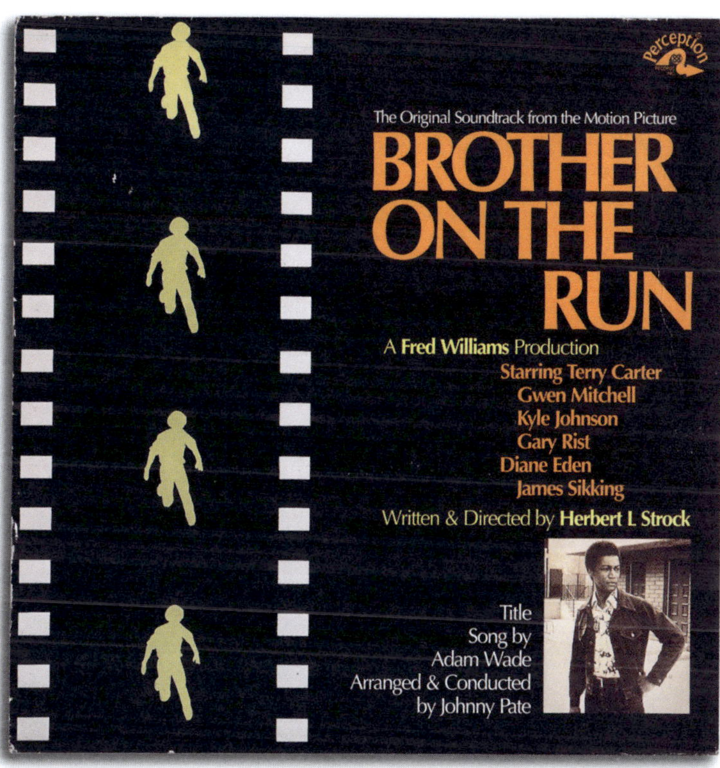

Brother On The Run
Johnny Pate
Perception, 1973
Herbert L. Strock (Director)
Fred Strak (Design)

17

MAR

Wild Style
Fab 5 Freddy, Fred Brathwaite
Animal Records, 1983
Charlie Ahearn (Director)

18

MAR

Star Trek - The Motion Picture
Jerry Goldsmith
Columbia Records, 1979
Robert Wise (Director)
Bob Peak (Design)

19

MAR

* Mar 20th, 1957 as Shelton Jackson "Spike" Lee
in Atlanta, Georgia, USA

Mo Better Blues
Branford Marsalis Quartet feat. Terence Blanchard
CBS Records, 1990
Spike Lee (Director)
Ken Kochman (Design)

20

MAR

Staying Alive
Various Artists
RSO, 1983
Sylvester Stallone (Director)
Bill Levy (Design)

21

MAR

FIVE MILES TO MIDNIGHT

UNITED ARTISTS

009 014

The 3rd Dimension

Original Soundtrack Recording
From The United Artists Picture
starring Sophia Loren and Anthony Perkins
Under The Direction of Anatole Litvak

Five Miles To Midnight
Mikis Theodorakis / Jaques Loussier
United Artists Records, 1966
Anatole Litvak (Director)

22 MAR

Quadrophenia
The Who
Polydor, 1979
Franc Roddam (Director)
Richard Evans (Design)

23

MAR

Hold On!
Herman's Hermits
MGM Records, 1966
Arthur Lubin (Director)
Ace Lehman (Design)

Signor Rossi
Franco Godi
Crippled Dick Hot Wax!, 1999
Bruno Bozzetto (Director)
Toner Van Bach (Design)

25

MAR

* Mar 26th, 1944 as Diana Ernestine Earle Ross
in Detroit, Michigan, USA

Mahagony
Michael Masser / Diana Ross
EMI Electrola, 1975
Berry Gordy (Director)
Bob Peak (Design)

26

MAR

* Mar 27th, 1963 as Quentin Jerome Tarantino
in Knoxville, Tennessee, USA

Pulp Fiction
Various Artists
MCA Records, 1994
Quentin Tarantino (Director)

27

MAR

Romeo & Julia
Nino Rota
Capitol Records, 1968
Franco Zeffirelli (Director)

28

MAR

GENERAL MUSIC ROME

ariola STEREO

MEIN NAME IST NOBODY

Original Film-Soundtrack IL MIO NOME E' NESSUNO

ENNIO MORRICONE

* Mar 29th, 1939 as Terence Hill as Mario Girotti
in Venice, Italia

Mein Name Ist Nobody
Ennio Morricone
General Music / Ariola Records, 1973
Tonino Valerii (Director)

Oklahoma
Al Goodman's Orchestra
Spin-O-Rama, 1955
Fred Zinnemann (Director)

† Mar 31th, 2008 as Julius Dassin in Athen, Greece

Phaedra
Mikis Theodorakis
United Artists Records, 1962
Jules Dassin (Director)

31

MAR

* Apr 1st, 1948 as Jimmy Cliff as James Chambers
in St. Catherine, Jamaica

The Harder They Come
Various Artists
Island Records, 1972
Perry Henzell (Director)
John Bryant (Design)

01

APR

* Apr 2nd, 1928 as Lucien Ginsburg in Paris, France

Les Chemins De Katmandou
Serge Gainsbourg / Jean-Claude Vannier
Finders Keepers Records, 2017
André Cayatte (Director)

02

APR

* Apr 3rd, 1922 as Doris Mary Ann Kappelhoff
in Cincinnati, Ohio, USA

Annie Get Your Gun
Franz Allers
CBS Records, 1963
Irving Townsend, Jim Foglesong (Director)
Isadore Seltzer, Push Pin Studios (Design)

03

APR

* Apr 4th, 1922 as Elmar Bernstein in New York City, USA

Cast A Giant Shadow
Elmer Bernstein
MCA Records, 1966
Melville Shavelson (Director)

04

APR

† Apr 5th, 2008 as Charlton Heston as John Charles Carter in Beverly Hills, California, USA

Airport 1975
John Cacavas
MCA Records, 1974
Jack Smight (Director)

05

APR

* Apr 6th, 1929 as Andres Ludwig Priwin
in Berlin, Germany

Irma La Douce
Andre Previn
United Artists Records, 1963
Billy Wilder (Director)

06

APR

* Apr 7th, 1939 as Francis Ford Coppola
in Detroit, Michigan, USA

Der Pate "The Godfather"
Nino Rota
Metronome, 1972
Francis Ford Coppola (Director)

07

APR

Rivers Edge
Various Artists
Roadrunner Records, 1987
Tim Hunter (Director)

08

APR

* Apr 9th, 1933 as Jean-Paul Belmondo
in Neuilly-sur-Seine, France

Der Profi
Ennio Morricone
WEA, 1981
Georges Lautner (Director)

09

APR

The Fox
Lalo Schifrin
Warner Bros. Records / Seven Arts Records, 1967
Mark Rydell (Director)
Ed Trasher (Design)

10

APR

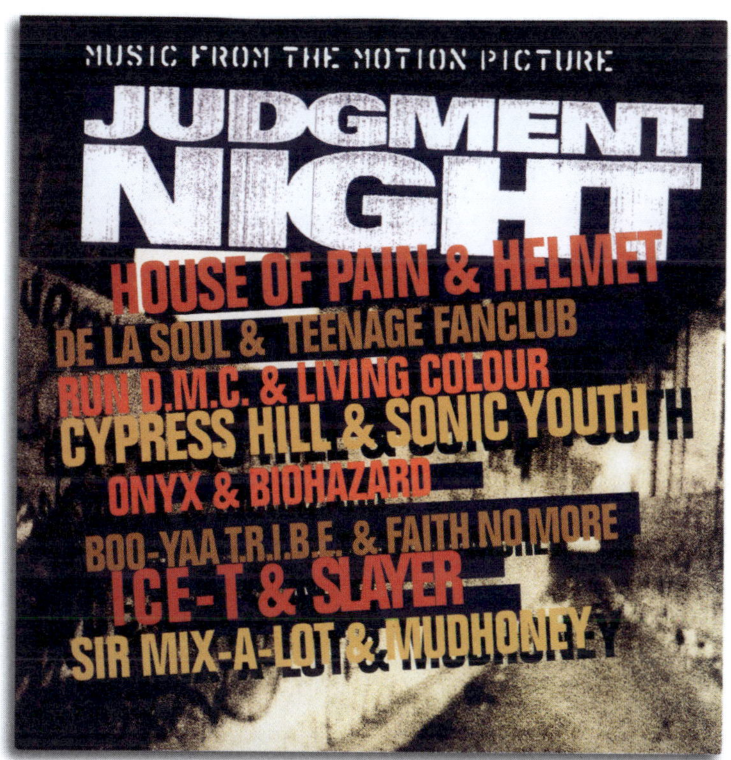

Judgment Night
Various Artists
Music On Vinyl, 1993
Stephen Hopkins (Director)
Mary Muarer (Design)

11

APR

* Apr 12th, 1946 as Liza May Minnelli
in Los Angeles, California, USA

Cabaret
Ralph Burns
Probe, 1972
Bob Fosse (Director)

* Apr 13th, 1940 as Vladimir Cosma in Bukarest, Romania

Diva
Vladimir Cosma
SPI Milan, 1981
Jean-Jacques Beiniex (Director)

13

APR

007 Thunderball
John Barry
United Artists Records, 1965
Terence Young (Director)

14

APR

* Apr 15th, 1917 as Gert Wilden as Gerhart Alfret Arnold Wychodil in Mährisch-Trübau, Austria

Schulmädchen Report
Gert Wilden & Orchestra
Crippled Dick Hot Wax!, 1996
Ernst Hofbauer (Director)
Tonmer Van Bach (Design)

15

APR

Django Unchained
Various Artists
Republic Records, 2013
Quentin Tarantino (Director)

16

APR

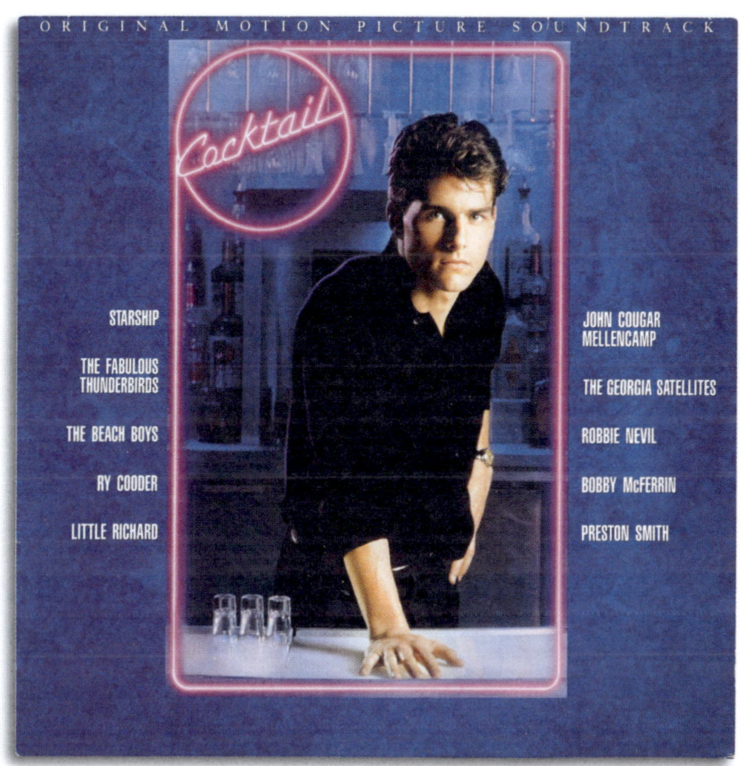

Cocktail
Various Artists
Elektra Records, 1988
Roger Donaldson (Director)
Richard Corman (Design)

* Apr 18th, 1974 as Friedrich Paravicini in Paris, France

Mr. Mandom
Friedrich Paravicini
Barnes & Quincy, 2011
Pencil Quincy (Design)

Singles
Various Artists
Warner Bros. Records, 1992
Cameron Crowe (Director)
Nancy Donald / David Coleman (Design)

19

APR

007 The Living Daylights
John Barry With a-ha & The Pretenders
Warner Bros. Records, 1987
John Glen (Director)
Mary Ann Dibs (Design)

20

APR

† Apr 21st, 2016 as Prince in Chanhassen, Minnesota, USA

Purple Rain
Prince
Warner Bros. Records, 1981
Albert Magnoli (Director)
Prince (Design)

21

APR

* Apr 22nd, 1937 as John Joseph Jack Nicholson
in Neptune City, New Jersey, USA

Einer Flog Über's Kuckucksnest
Jack Nitzsche
Fantasy Records, 1975
Milos Forman (Director)

22

APR

Hairspray
Various Artists
MCA Records, 1988
John Waters (Director)
Jeff Adamoff (Design)

* Apr 24th, 1942 as Barbara Streisand as Barbara Joan Streisand in New York City, USA

Yentl
Michel Legrand
CBS Records, 1983
Barbra Streisand (Director)
Allan Taylor (Design)

24

APR

* Apr 25th, 1940 as Alfredo James "Al" Pacino
in New York, USA

Sea Of Love
Trevor Jones
Mercury Records, 1989
Harold Becker (Director)
Nausica Loukakos (Design)

25

APR

* Apr 26th, 1940 as Giovanni Giorgio Moroder
in St. Ulrich, Gröden, Italy

Metropolis
Various Artists
CBS Records, 1984
Fritz Lang (Director)
Tom Nikosey/Los Angeles (Design)

26

APR

Sweet Charity
Cy Coleman
MCA Records, 1969
Bob Fosse (Director)
Bob Mcginnis (Design)

27

APR

Le Corps De Mon Ennemi
Francis Lai
WIP Records, 1976
Henri Verneuil (Director)
Vincent Rossel (Design)

28

APR

ORIGINAL SOUNDTRACK ALBUM FEATURING THE SANDPIPERS (COURTESY OF A&M RECORDS) AND THE STRAWBERRY ALARM CLOCK (COURTESY OF UNI RECORDS)

20th CENTURY FOX RECORDS

Beyond the Valley of the Dolls

COMPOSED AND CONDUCTED BY STU PHILLIPS

TFS 4211 STEREO

Beyond The Valley Of The Dolls
Stu Phillips & The Sandpipers
20th Century Fox Records, 1970
Russ Meyer (Director)

29

APR

† Apr 30th, 1989 as Sergio Leone in Rome, Italy

Es War Einmal In Amerika
Ennio Morricone
Mercury Records, 1984
Sergio Leone (Director)

* May 1st, 1969 as Wesley Wales "Wes" Anderson
in Houston, Texas, USA

The Darjeeling Limited
Various Artists
ABKCO Music & Records, 2007
Wes Anderson (Director)
Brian Fitzpatrick (Design)

01

MAY

2010
David Shire
A&M Records, 1984
Peter Hyams (Director)
Chuck Beeson (Design)

02

MAY

* May 3rd, 1933 as James Joseph Brown Jr.
in Barnwell, South Carolina, USA

Slaughters's Big Rip-Off
James Brown
Polydor, 1973
Gourdon Douglas (Director)

03

MAY

Indiana Jones & The Temple Of Doom
John Williams
Polydor Records, 1984
Steven Spielberg (Director)

04

MAY

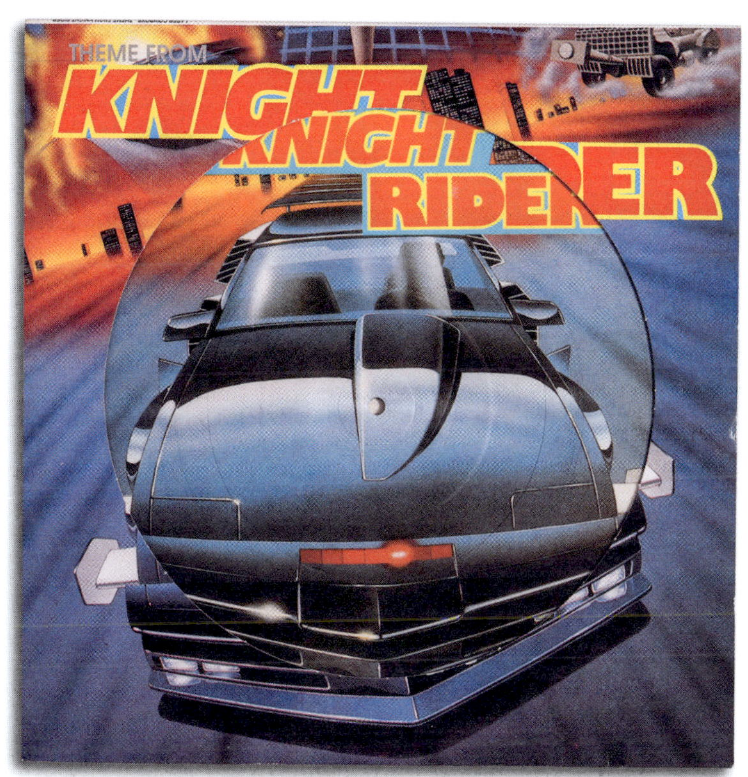

Theme From Knight Rider
Laser Cowboys
Italoheat, 1987
Glen A. Larson (Director)

05

MAY

La Boum Die Fete
Vladimir Costa
Polydor, 1981
Claude Pinoteau (Director)

Eat The Rich
Motörhead
GWR Records, 1987
Peter Richardson (Director)
Hunt Emerson (Design)

07

MAY

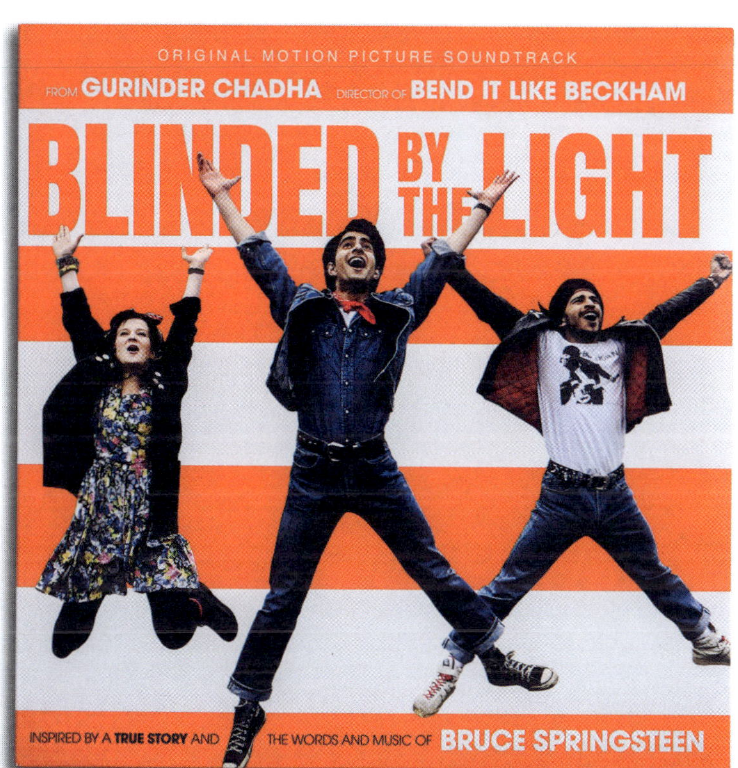

Blinded By The Light
Bruce Springsteen
Columbia Records, 2019
Gurinder Chadha (Director)

08

MAY

Dollar
Quincy Jones
Reprise Records, 2001
Richard Brooks (Director)
Don Weller (Design)

09

MAY

Lean On Me
Various Artists
Warner Bros. Records, 1989
John G. Avildsen (Director)

10

MAY

Delusion
Barry Adamson
Mute Records, 1991
Carl Colpaert (Director)

11

MAY

STEREO
A&M RECORDS
SP 4227

ORIGINAL SCORE COMPOSED AND CONDUCTED BY
Burt Bacharach
FROM THE 20th CENTURY-FOX PRODUCTION STARRING

PAUL NEWMAN
ROBERT REDFORD AND
KATHARINE ROSS IN
BUTCH CASSIDY AND
THE SUNDANCE KID

A GEORGE ROY HILL-PAUL MONASH PRODUCTION

* May 12th, 1928 as Burt Bacharach
in Kansas City, Missouri, USA

Butch Cassidy And The Sundance Kid
Burt Bacherach
A & M Records, 1969
George Roy Hill (Director)

* May 13th, 1912 as Gil Evans in Toronto, Ontario, Canada

Absolute Beginners
Various Artists & Gil Evans
Virgin Records, 1986
Julien Temple (Director)

13

MAY

Das Boot
Klaus Doldinger
WEA, 1981
Wolfgang Petersen (Director)

14

MAY

The Last Emperor
Ryuichi Sakamoto & David Byrne
Virgin Records, 1987
Bernardo Bertolucci (Director)
Vic Fair (Design)

15

MAY

Ghostbusters II
Various Artists
MCA Records, 1989
Ivan Reitman (Director)

16

MAY

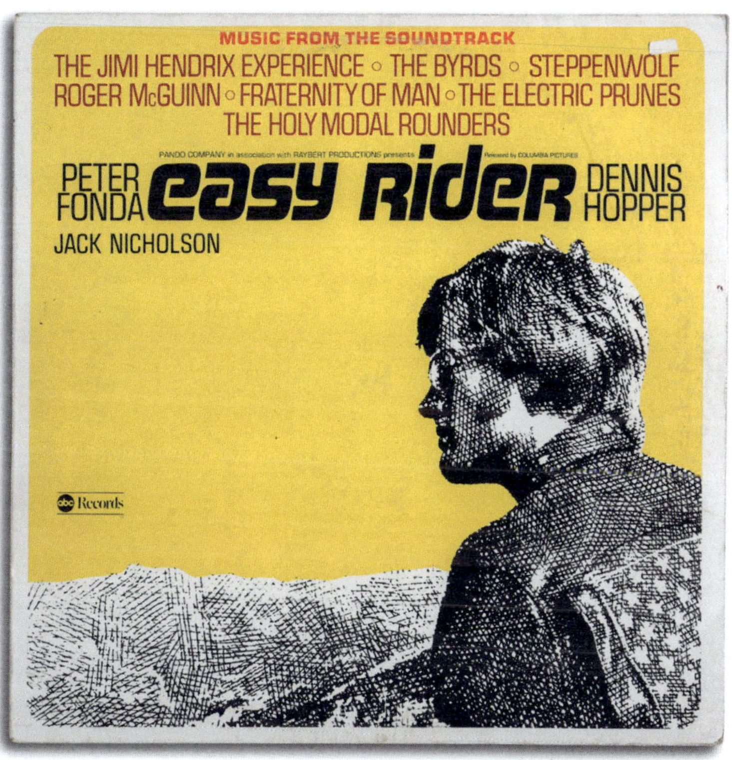

* May 17th, 1936 as Dennis Lee Hopper
in Dodge City, Kansas, USA

Easy Rider
Various Artists
ABC / Dunhill Records, 1969
Dennis Hopper (Director)

* May 18th, 1949 as Rick Wakeman in Middlesex, London, UK

Lisztomania
Rick Wakeman
A&M Records, 1975
Ken Russell (Director)
Roland Young (Design)

18

MAY

* May 19th, 1925 as Malcom Little in Omhah, Nebraska, USA

Malcolm X
Various Artists
Warner Bros. Records, 1972
Arnold Perl, Marvin Worth (Director)
Alan Sekuler, Ruby Mazur (Design)

19

MAY

* May 20th, 1932 as Dieter Rams in Wiesbaden, Germany

Brian Eno
RAMS – Original Soundtrack
UMC, 2020
Gary Hustwit (Director)
Gary Hustwit (Photo)

20

MAY

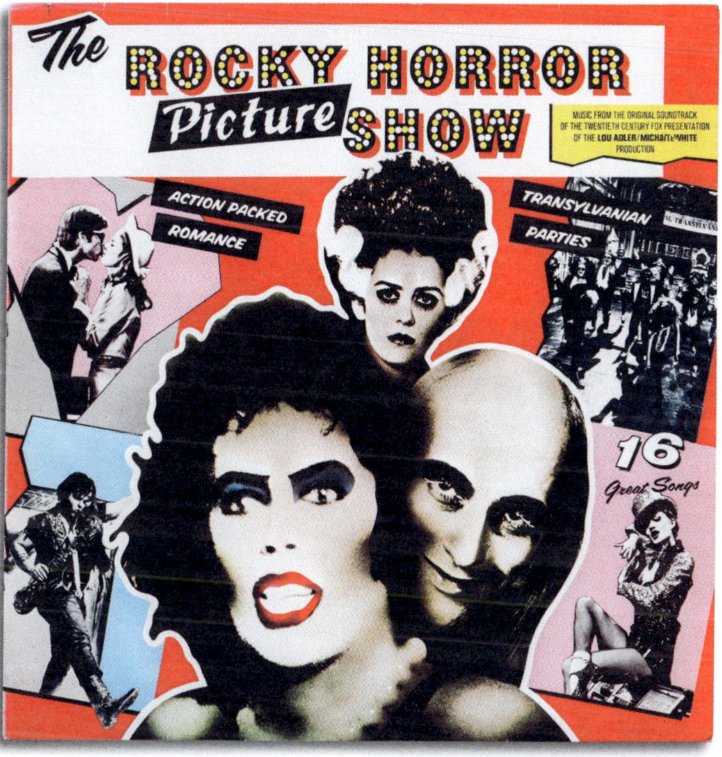

The Rocky Horror Picture Show
Various Artists
Green Line Records, 1989
Jim Sharman (Director)
John Pasche, Gull Graphics (Design)

Round Midnight
Herbie Hancock
CBS Records, 1986
Bertrand Tavernier (Director)

* May 23rd, 1933 as Joan Henrietta Collins in London, UK

The Stud
Various Artists
EMI Electrola, 1978
Quentin Masters (Director)
Alan Barlow (Design)

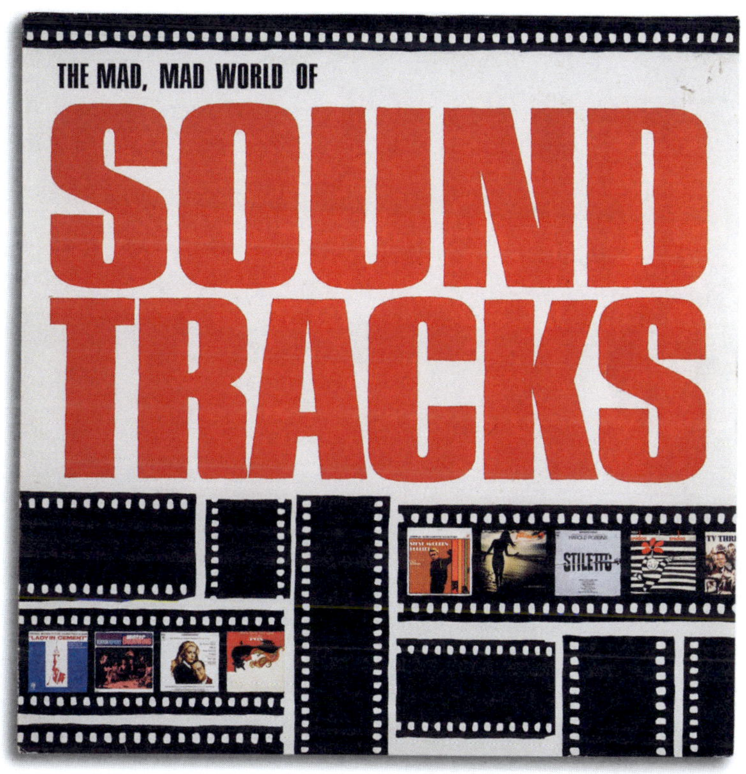

The Mad, Mad World Of Soundtracks
Various Artists
Motor Music, 1997
Stefan Kassel & Jens Bartoschek (Design)

24

MAY

Cotton Comes To Harlem
Galt MacDermot
United Artists Records, 1970
Ossie Davis (Director)
Bob Mcginnis (Design)

25

MAY

* May 26th, 1926 as Bruno Nicolai in Rome, Italia

Agente Speciale Operazione Remida
Bruno Nicolai
Dagored, 1999
Jess Franco (Director)
Roberto Zamori (Design)

26

MAY

Spiel Mir Das Lied Vom Tod
Ennio Morricone
Ariola, 1978
Sergio Leone (Director)

27

MAY

The Original Motion Picture Soundtrack Performed by Gladys Knight & the Pips

GLADYS KNIGHT in "PIPE DREAMS"

BUDDAH

* May 28th, 1944 as Gladys Maria Knight
in Atlanta, Georgia, USA

Pipe Dreams
Gladys Knight & The Pips
Buddah Records, 1976
Stephen F. Verona (Director)

28

MAY

† May 29th, 1982 as Romy Schneider in Paris, France

Clair De Femme
Jean Musy
Riviera LM Recording System, 1979
Costa-Gavras (Director)
Ferracci (Design)

29

MAY

Straight To Hell
Various Artists
Hell Records, 1987
Alex Cox (Director)
Blair Drawson (Design)

* May 31th, 1945 as Rainer Maria Fassbinder
in Bad Wörishofen, Germany

Lili Marleen
Peer Raben
Philips, 1980
Rainer Maria Fassbinder (Director)

31

MAY

* Jun 1st, 1935 as Paul Rudolf Parsifal Adlon in Munich, Germany

Out Of Rosenheim
Bob Telson
Papagayo, 1988
Percy Adlon (Director)
Renato Chesaro (Design)

01

JUN

Exorcist II – The Heretic
Ennio Morricone
Warner Bros. Records, 1977
John Boorman (Director)
Dan Perri (Design)

02

JUN

† Jun 3rd, 2016 as Cassius Marcellus Clay
in Scottsdale, Arizona, USA

The Greatest
Mandrill / Michael Masser / George Benson
Arista, 1977
Tom Gries (Director)

03

JUN

Day Of Anger
Riz Ortolani
Universal, 1967
Tonino Valerii (Director)

04 JUN

Grease 2
Various Artists
RSO, 1982
Patricia Birch (Director)

05

JUN

* Jun 6th, 1875 as Paul Thomas Mann in Lübeck, Germany

Death In Venice
Gustav Mahler
Deutsche Grammophon, 1967
Luchino Visconti (Director)

06

JUN

The Sting
Marvin Hamlisch & Scott Joplin
MCA Records, 1974
George Roy Hill (Director)
Chester Maydole (Design)

07

JUN

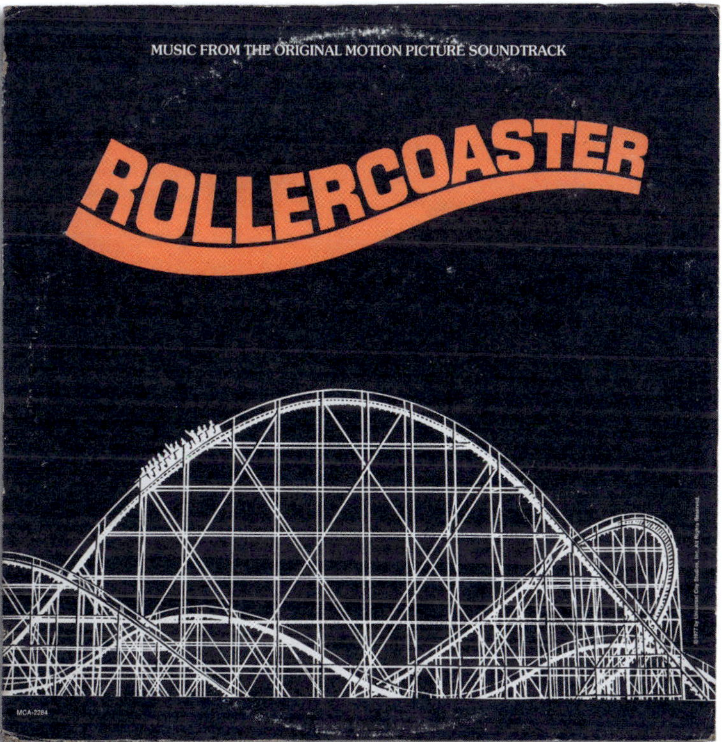

MUSIC FROM THE ORIGINAL MOTION PICTURE SOUNDTRACK

ROLLERCOASTER

Rollercoaster
Lalo Schifrin
MCA Records, 1977
James Goldstone (Director)

08

JUN

* Jun 9th, 1961 as Michael J. Fox in Edmonton, Alberta, Canada

Back To The Future
Various Artitsts
MCA Records, 1985
Robert Zemeckis (Director)

09

JUN

Für Ein Paar Dollar Mehr
Ennio Morricone
RCA Victor, 1966
Sergio Leone (Director)

10

JUN

† Jun 11th, 1979 as John Wayne as Marion Robert Morrison
in Los Angeles, California, USA

The Alamo
Dimitri Tiomkin
Philips, 1960
John Wayne (Director)

11

JUN

Midnight Express
Giorgio Moroder
Casablanca Records, 1978
Alan Parker (Director)
Gribitt ! (Design)

12

JUN

The Wanderers
Various Artists
RCA Victor, 1979
Philip Kaufman (Director)

13

JUN

MUSIC FROM THE ORIGINAL SOUND TRACK
VISIONS OF EIGHT
COMPOSED AND CONDUCTED BY
HENRY MANCINI

DAVID L. WOLPER presents a film by
MILOS FORMAN · KON ICHIKAWA · CLAUDE LELOUCH
JURI OZEROV · ARTHUR PENN · MICHAEL PFLEGHAR
JOHN SCHLESINGER · MAI ZETTERLING (in alphabetical order)
Produced by Stan Margulies · Executive Producer: David L. Wolper · Technicolor
RCA

† Jun 14th, 1994 as Henry Mancini as Enrico Nicola Mancini
in Beverly Hills, California, USA

Visions Of Eight
Henri Mancini
RCA Victor, 1973
Milos Forman & Others (Director)

14

JUN

Raumpatrouille Orion
Peter-Thomas-Sound-Orchester
Fontana, 1979
Theo Mezger, Michael Braun (Director)

15

JUN

THE ORIGINAL SOUND TRACK ALBUM

2315 282

MGM Presents

WESTWORLD

Music Composed, Conducted & Arranged by FRED KARLIN

MGM RECORDS

* Jun 16th, 1936 as Frederick James Karlin
in Chicago, Illinois, USA

Westworld
Fred Karlin
MGM Records, 1973
Michael Crichton (Director)

16

JUN

* Jun 17th, 1931 as Dominic Frotniere
in New Haven, Connecticut, USA

Hang Em High
Dominic Frontiere
United Artists, 1968
Tzed Post (Director)

17

JUN

Yellow Submarine
The Beatles
Apple Records, 1969
George Dunning (Director)
Robert Balser, George Dunning, Jack Stokes (Design)

18

JUN

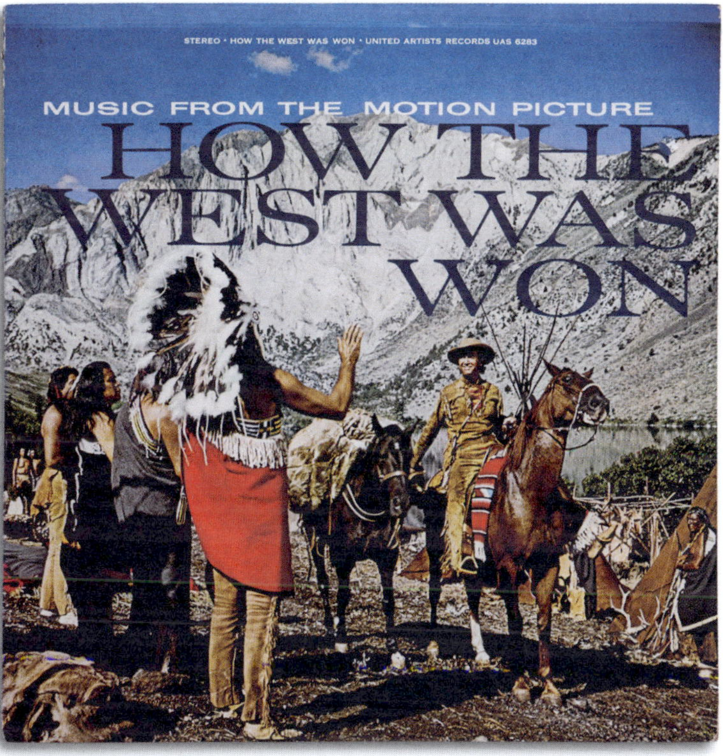

How The West Was Won
Alfred Newman, Debbie Reynolds, Ken Darby
MGM Records, 1963
Henry Hathaway, John Ford Und George Marshall (Director)

American Gigolo
Giorgio Moroder
Polydor Records, 1980
Paul Schrader (Director)

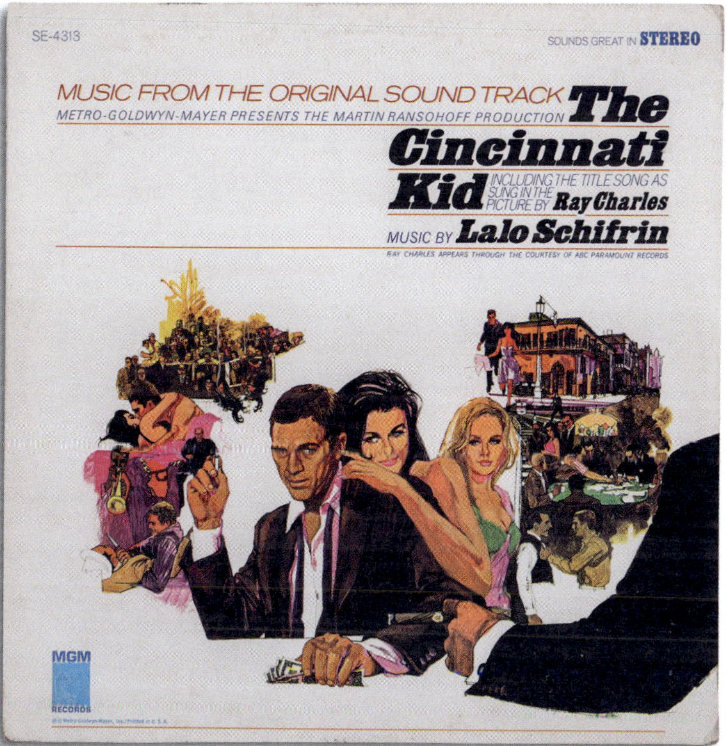

* Jun 21st, 1932 as Boris Claudio Schifrin
in Buenos Aires, Argentina

The Cincinnati Kid
Lalo Schifrin
MGM Records, 1965
Norman Jewison (Director)

The Pink Panther
Henri Mancini
Cine Music, 1983
Blake Edwards (Director)

22

JUN

Trouble Man
Marvin Gaye
Tamla Motown, 1972
Ivan Dixon (Director)

23

JUN

Rambo 2. Teil Der Auftrag First Blood Part 2
Jerry Goldsmith
Colosseum Schallplatten, 1985
George P. Cosmatos (Director)
Scotia Deutschland Filmverleih (Design)

24

JUN

Ziggy Stardust And The Spiders From Mars
David Bowie
RCA Victor, 1983
D. A. Pennebaker (Director)
Alexander Da'Lama (Design)

25

JUN

Mary Poppins
R.M Sherman, R.B. Sherman
Ducheese, 1964
Robert Stevenson (Director)

26

JUN

† Jun 27th, 2014 as Robert "Bobby" Dwayne Womack
in Los Angles, Califonia, USA

110th Street
Bobby Womack
United Artists Records, 1972
Barry Shear (Director)

27

JUN

* Jun 28th, 1926 as Mel Brooks as Melvin Kaminsky
in Brooklyn, NYC, USA

To Be Or Not To Be
Lionel Conway & Roger Watson
Island Records, 1983
Alan Johnson (Director)

28

JUN

M*A*S*H
Johnny Mandel
Columbia Records, 1970
Robert Altman (Director)

High Fidelity
Various Artists
Hollywood Records, 2000
Stephen Frears (Director)
Jkemper (Design)

30

JUN

...visual sound STEREO LOS 17001

LIBERTY

MARLON BRANDO
KARL MALDEN

PARAMOUNT PICTURES Presents ORIGINAL SOUND TRACK From the Motion Picture

ONE EYED JACKS

Music by
HUGO FRIEDHOFER

† Jul 1st, 2004 as Marlon Brando
in Los Angeles, California, USA

One Eyed Jacks
Hugo Friedhofer
Liberty Records, 1961
Marlon Brando (Director)

01

JUL

† Jul 2nd, 1997 as James "Jimmy" Maitland Stewart
in Beverly Hills, California, USA

Born To Dance
Various Artists – Seven Cole Porter
Classic International Filmusicals, 1936
Roy Del Ruth (Director)

02

JUL

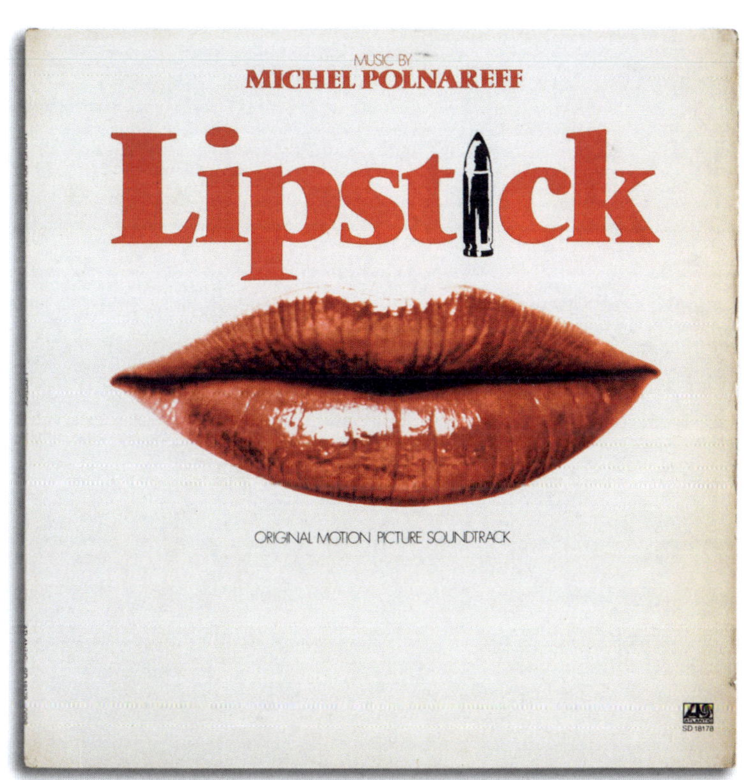

* Jul 3rd, 1944 as Michel Polnareff in Nérac, France

Lipstick
Michel Polnareff
Atlantic Records, 1976
Lamont Johnson (Director)

03

JUL

Stiletto
Sid Ramin
Columbia Records, 1969
Bernard Kowalski (Director)

04

JUL

Etat De Siege
Mikis Theodorakis
CBS Records, 1973
Costa-Gavras (Director)

* Jul 6th, 1946 as Sylvester Enzio "Sly" Stallone
in New York City, USA

Rocky III
Bill Conti
Liberty Records, 1982
Sylvester Stallone (Director)

06

JUL

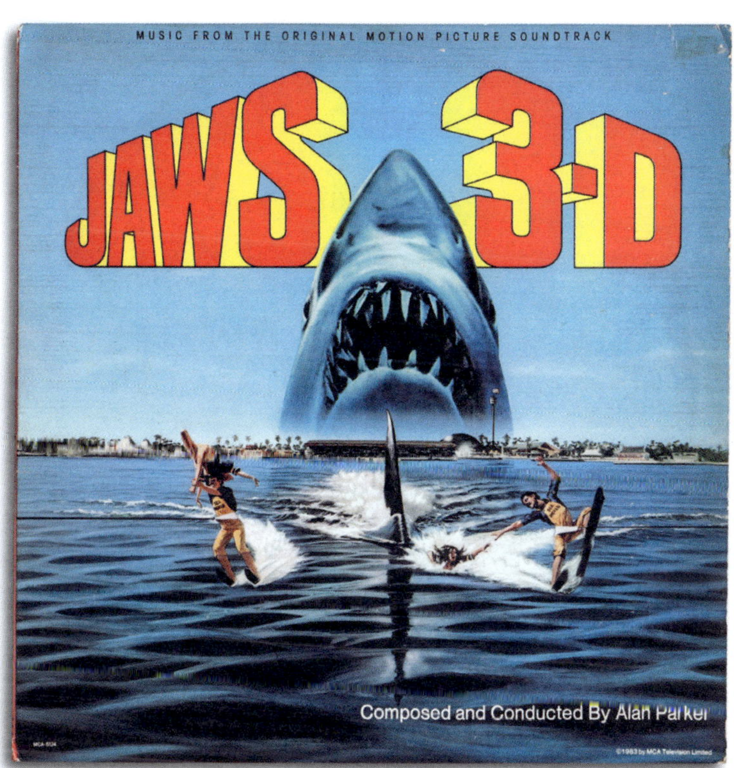

Jaws 3D
Alan Parker
MCA Records, 1982
Joe Alves (Director)

07

JUL

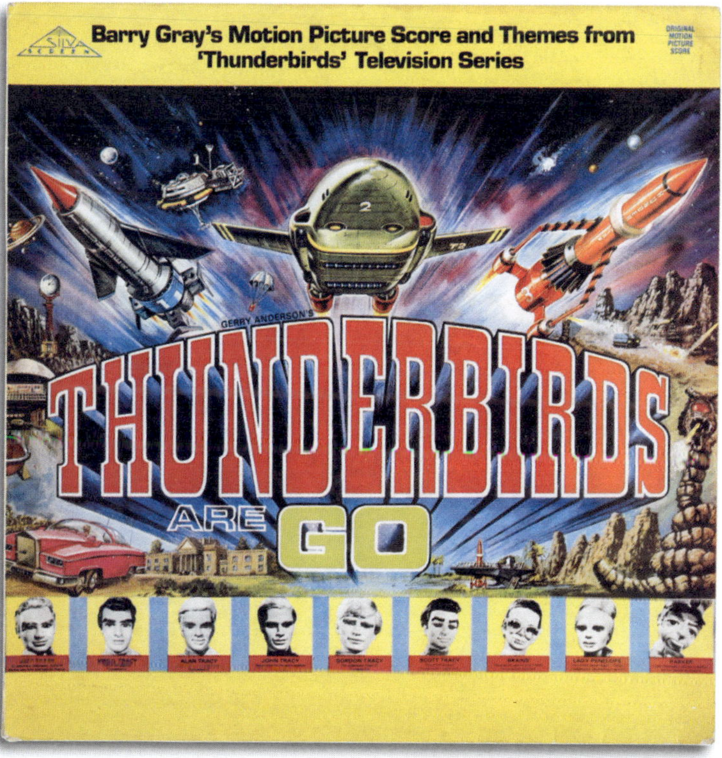

Thunderbirds Are Go
Barry Gray
Silva Screen Records, 1967
David Lane (Director)

Marco Polo
Ennio Morricone
Ariola, 1982
Giuliano Montaldo (Director)

09

JUL

* Jul 10th, 1947 as Arlo Guthrie in Brooklyn, NYC, USA

Alice's Restaurant
Arlo Guthrie
Reprise Records, 1969
Arthur Penn (Director)
Ed Trasher (Design)

10

JUL

La Boum 2
Vladimir Cosma
Polydor Records, 1982
Claude Pinoteau (Director)
Philippe Lemoine (Design)

11

JUL

Tommy By The Who
Various Artists
Polydor Records, 1975
Ken Russell (Director)
The Robert Stigwood Organisation (Design)

12

JUL

* Jul 13th, 1942 as Harrison Ford in Chicago, Illinois, USA

Der Einzige Zeuge
Maurice Jarre
Colosseum Schallplatten, 1985
Peter Weir (Director)

13

JUL

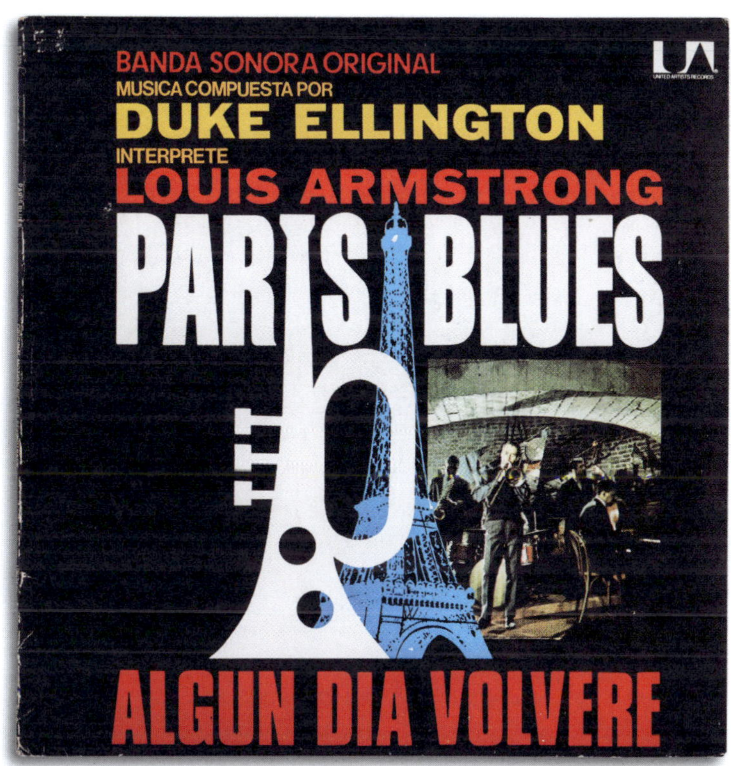

Paris Blues
Duke Ellington
United Artists Records, 1961
Martin Ritt (Director)

14

JUL

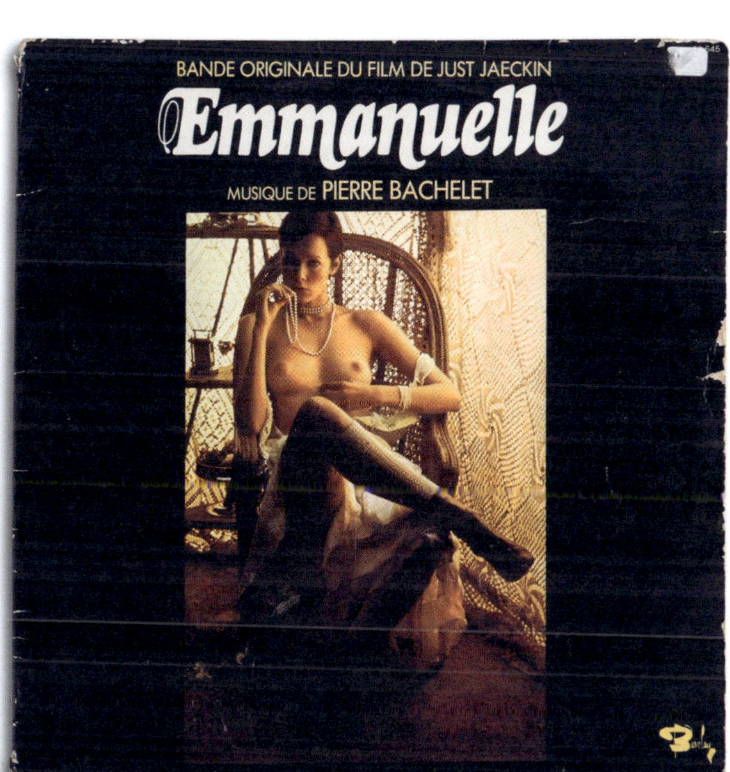

Emmanuelle
Piere Bachelet
Barclay, 1974
Just Jaeckin (Director)
Francis Giacobetti (Design)

15

JUL

Doctor Zhivago
Maurice Jarre
MGM Records, 1965
David Lean (Director)

16

JUL

* Jul 17th, 1958 as Wong Kar-Wai in Shanghai, China

In The Mood For Love
Various Artists
Universal Music, 2016
Wong Kar-Wai (Director)

17

JUL

The Great Escape
Elmer Bernstein
United Artists Records, 1963
John Sturges (Director)
Frank C. McCarthy (Design)

18

JUL

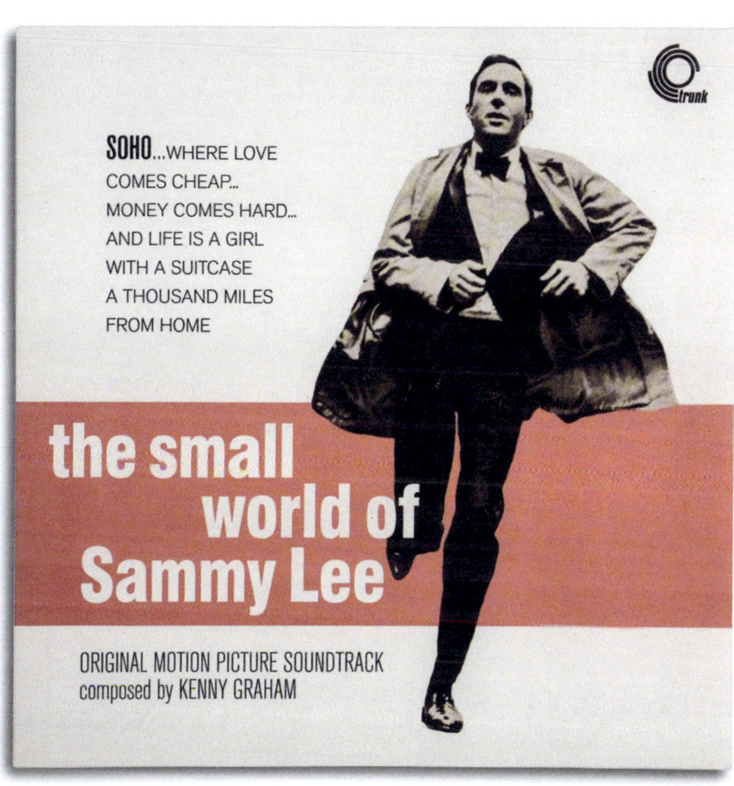

* Jul 19th, 1924 as Kenny Graham as Kenneth Thomas Skingle in London, UK

The Small World Of Sammy Lee
Kenny Graham
Trunk Records, 2013
Ken Hughes (Director)

† Jul 20th, 1973 as Bruce Lee as Lee-Jun-Fan in Hongkong

Bruce Lee's Game Of Death
John Barry
Dagored, 2000
Robert Clouse (Director)

20

JUL

† Jul 21st, 2004 as Jerrald "Jerry" King Goldsmith
in Beverly Hills, Los Angeles, USA

Logan's Run
Jerry Goldsmith
MGM Records, 1976
Michael Anderson (Director)

21

JUL

The Magnificent Seven – "Return Of The Seven"
Elmer Bernstein
Liberty Records, 1966
Burt Kennedy (Director)

22 JUL

INCLUDES ORIGINAL FILM SCORE BY ANTONIO PINTO
AND CLASSIC AMY WINEHOUSE TRACKS

THE ORIGINAL SOUNDTRACK

AMY

† Jul 23rd, 2011 as Amy Jade Winehouse
in Camden, London, UK

Amy
Antonio Pinto, Amy Winehouse
Island Records, 2015
Asif Kapadia (Director)

23

JUL

† Jul 24th, 1980 as Peter Sellers as Richard Henry Sellers in London, UK

The Party
Henri Mancini
RCA Victor, 1968
Blake Edwards (Director)
Jack Davies (Design)

24

JUL

The Sandpebbles
Jerry Goldsmith
20th Century Fox Records, 1966
Robert Wise (Director)

ORIGINAL MOTION PICTURE SOUND TRACK
WARNER BROS. PRESENTS
PERFORMANCE
STARRING
JAMES FOX - MICK JAGGER
A GOODTIMES ENTERPRISES PRODUCTION
MUSIC BY JACK NITZSCHE
"MEMO FROM TURNER" PERFORMED BY MICK JAGGER
"GONE DEAD TRAIN" SUNG BY RANDY NEWMAN
STEREO
WB
BS 2554

* Jul 26th, 1943 as Sir Michael Philip Jagger
in Dartford Kent, England, UK

Performance
Various Artists
Warner Bros. Records, 1970
Nicolas Roeg, Donald Cammell (Director)
Ed Trasher (Design)

26

JUL

Il Était Une Fois Dans L'Ouest
Ennio Morricone
RCA Gala, 1971
Sergio Leone (Director)

Wattstax – The Living Word
Various Artists
Stax Records, 1972
Mel Stuart (Director)
Wilkes & Braun Inc. (Design)

28

JUL

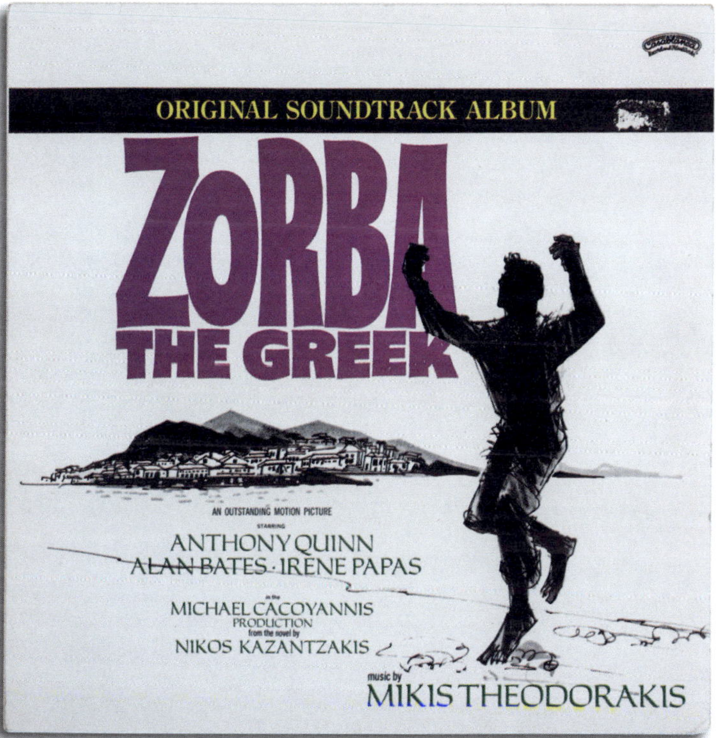

* Jul 29th, 1925 as Mikis Thodorakis on Island Chios, Greece

Zorba, The Greek
Mikis Theodorakis
Casablanca Records, 1973
Michael Cacoyannis (Director)

Flashdance
Various Artists
Polygram, 1983
Adrian Lye (Director)

30

JUL

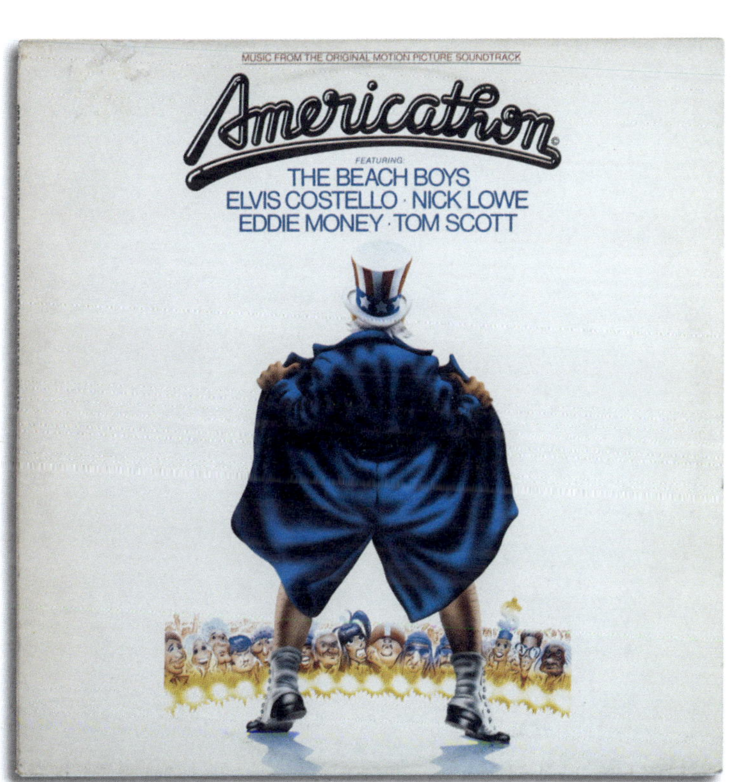

Americathon
Various Artists
CBS Records, 1979
Neil Israel (Director)

The Adventures
Antonio Carlos Jobim
Paramount Records, 1970
Lewis Gilbert (Director)

01

AUG

† Aug 2nd, 1997 as William S. Burroughs
in Lawrence, Kansas, USA

Drugstore Cowboy
Elliot Goldenthal
Novrus Records, 1989
Gus Van Sant (Director)
Pietro Alfieri (Design)

02

AUG

Body Love
Klaus Schulze
Ariola, 1977
Lasse Braun (Director)
Charles Mikael Liege (Design)

03

AUG

* Aug 4th, 1901 as Louis Daniel "Satchmo" Armstrong
in New Orleans, Louisiana, USA

High Society
Louis Armstrong
Capitol Records, 1956
Charles Walters (Director)
Jim Jonson (Design)

04

AUG

† Aug 5th, 1962 as Norma Jeane Baker
in Los Angeles, California, USA

Some Like It Hot
Various Artists
United Artists Records, 1959
Billy Wilder (Director)
Stephen Haas (Design)

05

AUG

The Quiller Memorandum
John Barry
Columbia Records, 1966
Michael Anderson (Director)

06

AUG

South Pacific
Rodgers & Hammerstein
RCA Victor, 1958
Joshua Logan (Director)

07

AUG

* Aug 8th, 1937 as Dustin Lee Hoffman
in Los Angeles, California, USA

Lenny
Dustin Hoffman, Ralph Burns
United Artists Records, 1974
Bob Fosse (Director)

08

AUG

Escalation
Ennio Morricone
Dagored, 2015
Roberto Faenza (Director)

09

AUG

† Oct 10th, 2008 as Alsaac Lee Hayes, Jr.
in Memphis, Tennessee, USA

Tough Guys
Isacc Hayes
Enterprise, 1974
Duccio Tessari (Director)
The Stax Organisation (Design)

10

AUG

† Aug 11th, 2014 as Robin McLaurin Williams
in Paradise Cay, California, USA

Good Morning, Vietnam
Various Artists
A & M Records, 1988
Barry Levinson (Director)
Stephen Vaughan (Design)

11

AUG

007 – A View To A Kill
John Barry With Duran Duran
EMI Records Ltd., 1985
John Glen (Director)

12

AUG

* Aug 13th, 1899 as Sir Alfred Joseph Hitchcock
in Leytonstone, UK

Psycho
Bernard Herrmann
Doxy, 2015
Alfred Hitchccok (Director)

13

AUG

She Had A Taste For Music
Various Artists
Dagored, 1999
Various (Director)

14

AUG

1969 Woodstock Music & Art Fair presents An Aquarian
Exposition – 3 Days of Peace & Music

Woodstock
Various Artists
Atlantic Records, 1970
Michael Wadleigh (Director)

15

AUG

† Aug 16th, 1977 as Elvis Aaron Presley
in Memphis, Tennessee, USA

Double Trouble
Elvis Presley
RCA Victor, 1967
Norman Taurog (Director)

16

AUG

* Aug 17th, 1943 as Robert Anthony De Niro, Jr.
in New York City. USA

Goodfellas
Various Artists
Atlantic, 1990
Martin Scorsese (Director)

17

AUG

* Aug 18th, 1936 as Charles Robert Redford, Jr.
in Santa Monica, California, USA

Out Of Africa
John Barry
MCA Records, 1986
Sydney Pollack (Director)

18

AUG

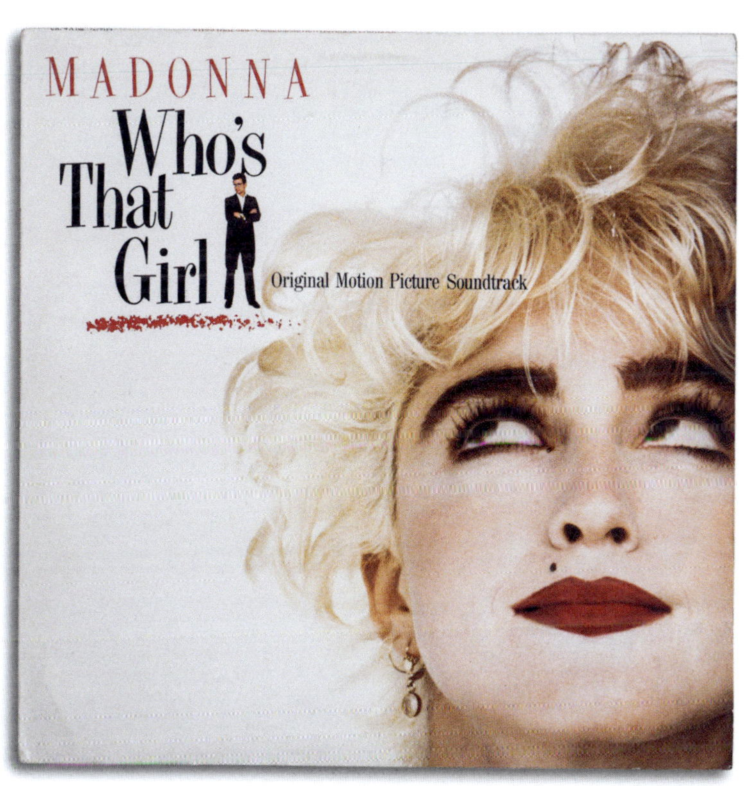

Who's That Girl
Madonna
Sire Records, 1987
James Foley (Director)

Shaft
Isaac Hayes
Stax Records, 1971
Gordon Parks (Director)
Tony Seiniger (Design)

20

AUG

Never On Sunday
Manos Hadjidakis
United Artists Records, 1960
Jules Dassin (Director)

21

AUG

Taxi Driver
Bernard Herrmann
Arista Records, 1976
Martin Scorsese (Director)

22

AUG

The Falcon And The Snowdown
Pat Metheny And Lyle Mays
EMI America, 1985
John Schlesinger (Director)
Henry Marquez (Design)

23

AUG

Porgy And Bess
George Gershwin
CBS Records, 1959
Otto Preminger (Director)

24

AUG

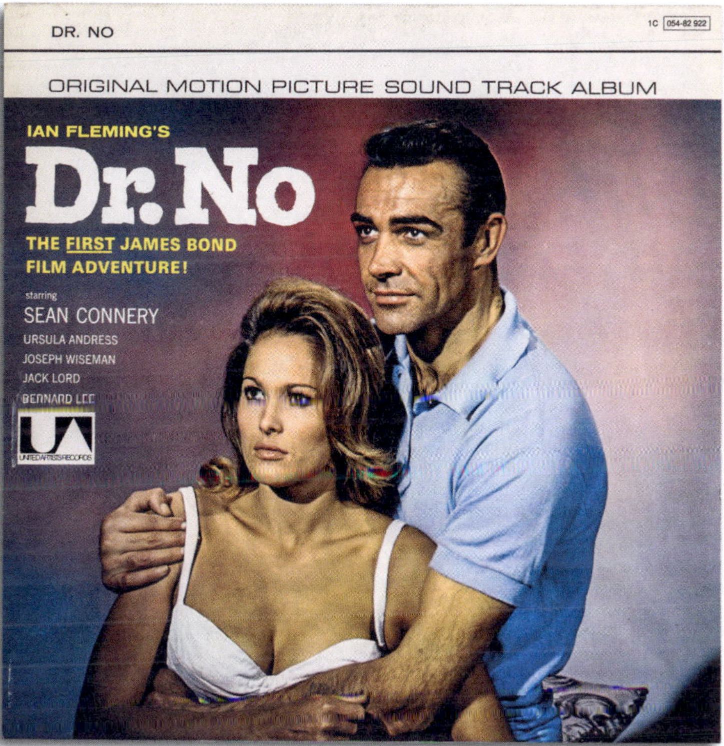

* Aug 25th, 1930 as Sir Thomas Sean Connery
in Edinburgh, Scotland

007 – Dr. No
Monty Norman
United Artists Records, 1965
Terence Young (Director)

25

AUG

Gandhi
Ravi Shankar, George Fenton
RCA Victor, 1982
Richard Attenborough (Director)

26

AUG

Claudine
Glady Knight & The Pips
Buddah Records, 1974
John Berry (Director)
Milton Sincoff (Design)

Spellbound
Miklos Rosza
Stanyan Record, 1974
Alfred Hitchcock (Director)
Hy Fujita (Design)

28

AUG

The Yellow Rolls-Royce
Riz Ortolani
MGM Records, 1965
Anthony Asquith (Director)

29

AUG

† Aug 30th, 2003 Charles Dennis Buchinsky
in Los Angeles, California, USA

Death Wish
Herbie Hancock
Columbia Records, 1974
Michael Winner (Director)

30

AUG

To Kill A Mockungbird
Elmer Bernstein
Citadel Records, 1981
Robert Mulligan (Director)

31

AUG

Lost Horizon
Burt Bacharach
Bell Records, 1973
Charles Jarrott (Director)
Beverly Weinstein (Design)

01

SEP

THE BEST OF Edgar Wallace

Original music from the German cult thrillers by

PETER THOMAS & MARTIN BÖTTCHER

The Best Of Edgar Wallace
Peter Thomas & Martin Böttcher
All Score Media, 2002
Edgar Wallace (Director)
Thomas Gross (Design)

02

SEP

The Man With The Golden Arm
Elmer Bernstein
Decca Records, 1956
Otto Preminger (Director)
Saul Bass (Design)

03

SEP

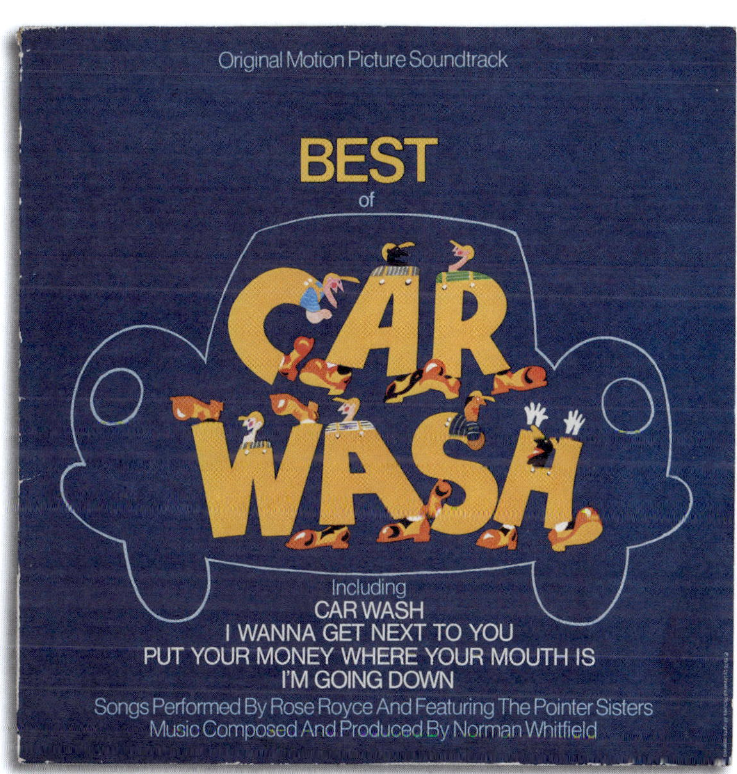

Car Wash
Norman Whitfield
MCA Records, 1976
Michael Schultz (Director)

04

SEP

* Sep 5th, 1942 as Werner Herzog Stipet in Munich, Germany

On The Way To A Little Way – Nosferatu
Popul Vuh
Egg, 1978
Werner Herzog (Director)

05

SEP

PERMANENT RECORD

JOE STRUMMER
& THE LATINO
ROCKABILLY WAR
Trash City
Baby The Trans
Nefertiti Rock
Nothin' 'Bout Nothin'
BODEANS
Waiting On Love

J.D. SOUTHER
Wishing On
Another Lucky Star
THE STRANGLERS
All Day And All
Of The Night

LOU REED
Something Happened
THE GODFATHERS
'Cause I Said So

MUSIC FROM THE
ORIGINAL MOTION PICTURE
SOUNDTRACK

Permanent Record
Various Artists
CBS Records, 1988
Marisa Silver (Director)

06 SEP

* Sep 7th, 1930 as Sunny Rollins in New York City, USA

Alfie
Sonny Rollins
Impulse !, 1966
Lewis Gilbert (Director)

† Sep 8th, 1991 as Alex North in Los Angeles, California, USA

Spartacus
Alex North
Decca Records, 1960
Stanley Kubrick (Director)

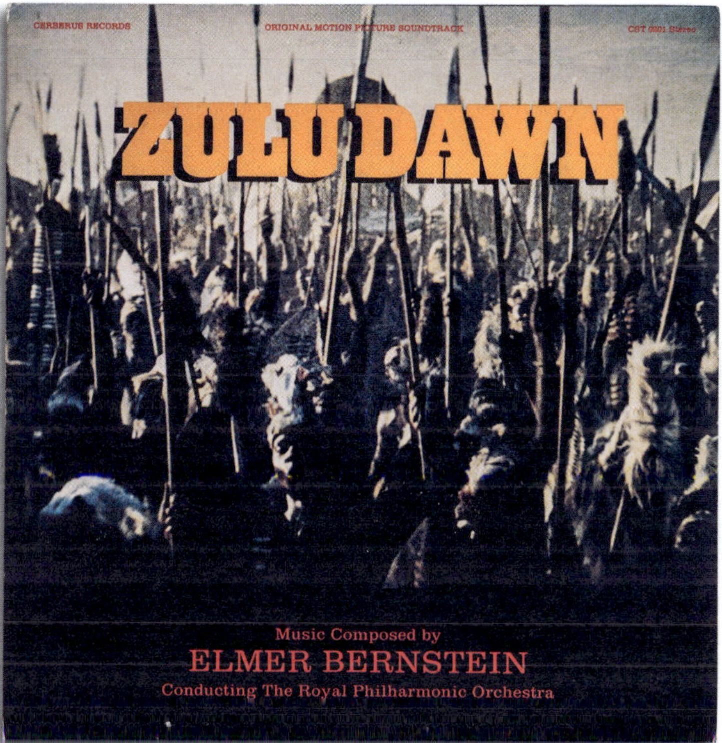

CERBERUS RECORDS
ORIGINAL MOTION PICTURE SOUNDTRACK

ZULU DAWN

Music Composed by
ELMER BERNSTEIN
Conducting The Royal Philharmonic Orchestra

Zulu Dawn
Elmer Bernstein
Cerberus Records, 1979
Douglas Hickox (Director)

Stardust
Various Artists
EMI Records Ltd., 1975
Michael Apted (Director)
Ken Hazelwood (Design)

10

SEP

Jonathan Livingston Seagull
Neil Diamond
CBS Records, 1971
Hall Bartlett (Director)
Ed Caraeff, David Larkham, Michael Ross (Design)

11

SEP

† Sep 12th, 2003 as Johnny Cash
in Nashville, Tennessee, USA

I Walk The Line
Johnny Cash
CBS Records, 1971
John Frankenheim (Director)

12

SEP

* Sep 13th, 1924 as Maurice Alexis Jarre in Lyon, France

Apology
Maurice Jarre
Varèse Sarabande, 1986
Robert Bierman (Director)
Sam Gimbel (Design)

13

SEP

† Sep 14th, 2009 as Patrick Wayne Swayze
in Los Angeles, California, USA

Dirty Dancing
Various Artists
RCA Records, 1987
Emile Ardolino (Director)

Help!
The Beatles
Parlophone, 1965
Richard Lester (Director)
Robert Freeman (Design)

15

SEP

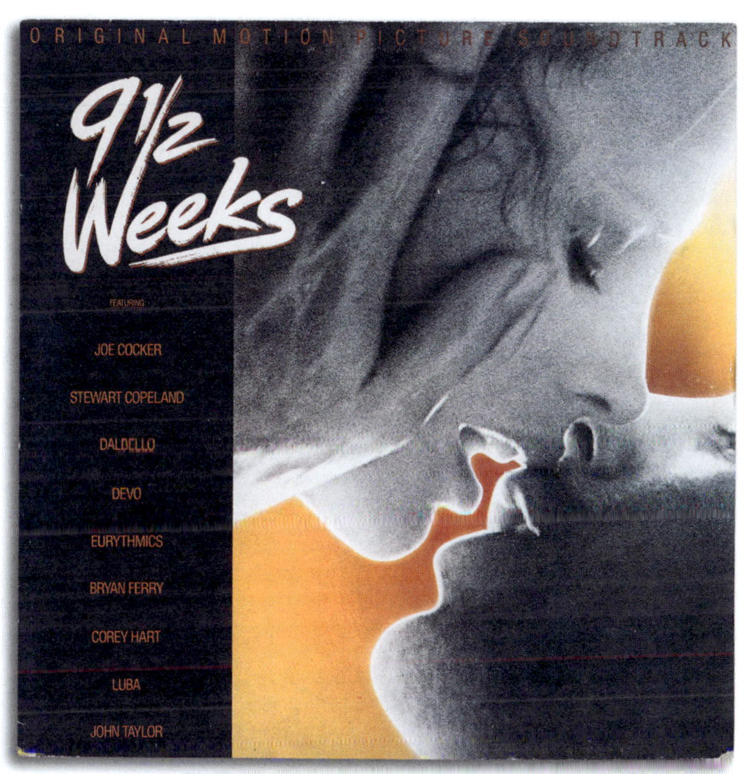

* Sep 16th, 1952 as Mickey Rourke in Schenectady, New York, USA

9 1/2 Weeks
Various Artists
Capitol Records, 1986
Adrian Lyne (Director)

16

SEP

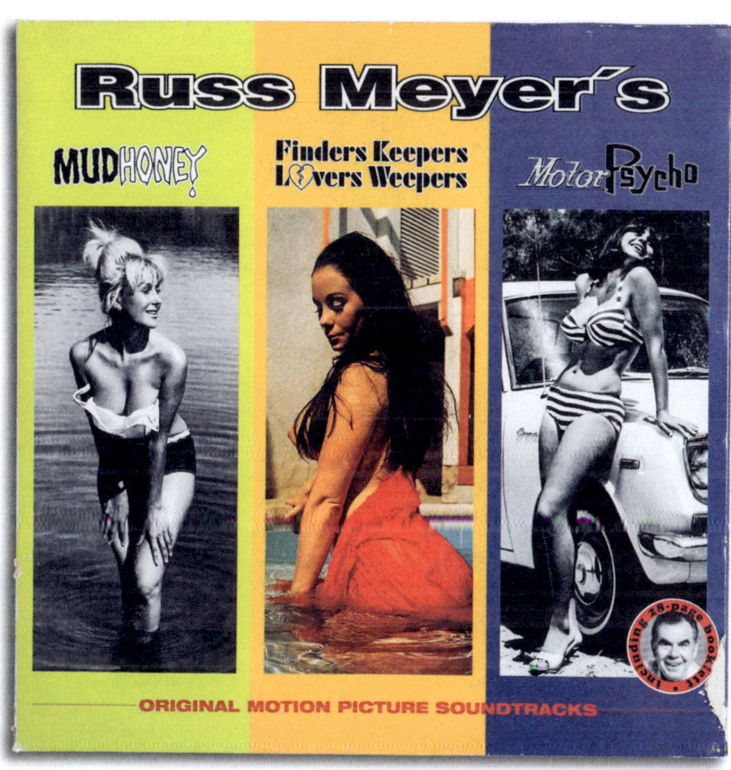

Russ Meyer's Mudhoney, Finders Keepers, Motorpsycho
Various Artists
Normal Records, 1995
Russ Meyer (Director)
Thomas Hartlage (Design)

17

SEP

* Sep 18th, 1970 as James Marshall "Jimi" Hendrix
in London, UK

Rainbow Bridge
Jimi Hendrix
Reprise Records, 1971
Chuck Wein (Director)

18

SEP

Heavy Metal
Various Artists
Full Moon Epic, 1981
Gerald Potterton (Director)

19

SEP

Rosemary's Baby
Christopher Komeda
Waxwork Records, 1968
Roman Polanski (Director)
Jay Shaw (Design)

20

SEP

* Sep 21st, 1950 as William James "Bill" Murray
in Wilmette, Illinois, USA

Scrooged
Various Artists
A&M Records, 1988
Richard Donner (Director)

21

SEP

Down By Law
John Lurie
Made To Measure, 1987
Jim Jarmuch (Director)

* Sep 23rd, 1930 as Raymond Charles Robinson
in Albany, Georgia, USA

In The Heat Of The Night
Quincy Jones
MGM Records, 1967
Norman Jewison (Director)

23

SEP

Lovers And Other Strangers
Fred Karlin
ABC Records, 1970
Cy Howard (Director)

24

SEP

The Warriors
Various Artists
A&M Records, 1979
Walter Hill (Director)

25

SEP

The Golden Voyage Of Sinbad
Miklos Rozsa
United Artists Records, 1974
Gordon Hessler (Director)

26

SEP

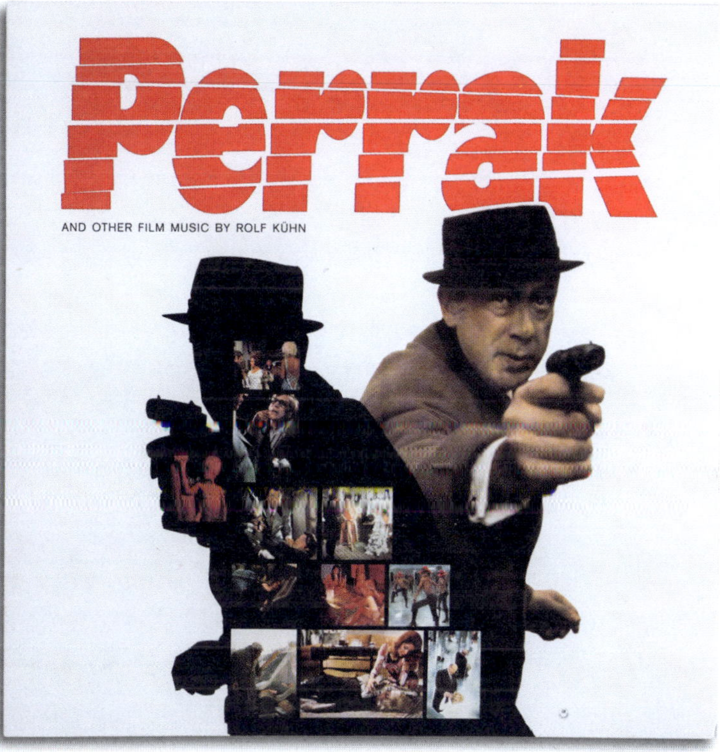

Perrak
Rolf Kühn
All Score Media, 2014
Alfred Vohrer (Director)
Weiss-Heiten (Design)

Go Trabbi Go
Various Artists
Hansa, 1990
Peter Timm (Director)
A. Härlin (Design)

ORIGINAL MOTION PICTURE SOUNDTRACK

GREAT BALLS OF FIRE!

NEWLY RECORDED PERFORMANCES BY JERRY LEE LEWIS

* Sep 29th, 1935 as Jerry Lee Lewis
in Ferriday, Louisiana, USA

Great Balls Of Fire
Jerry Lee Lewis
Polydor Records, 1989
Jim McBride (Director)
Michael Bays And Giulio Turturro (Design)

† Sep 30th, 1955 as James Byron Dean
in Cholame, California, USA

The James Dean Story
Leith Stevens
Capitol Records, 1957
Robert Altman (Director)
David Stone Martin (Design)

American Graffiti Vol. 3
Various Artists
MCA Records, 1976
George Lucas (Director)
Elliot Gilbert & L. Marmorstein (Design)

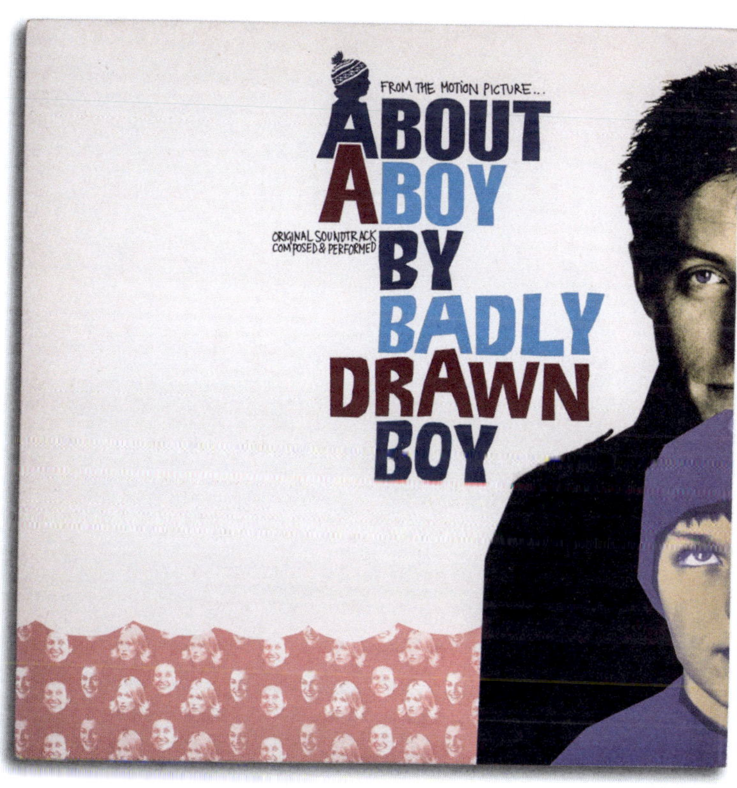

* Oct 2nd, 1969 as Badly Drawn Boy as Damon Michael Gough
in Manchester, UK

About A Boy
Badly Drawn Boy
XL Recordings, 2002
Chris Weitz, Paul Weitz (Director)
Andy Votel (Design)

02

OCT

Iron Eagle
Various Artists
EMI Records Ltd., 1986
Sidney J. Furie (Director)

03

OCT

My Fair Lady
Audrey Hepburn, Rex Harrison
CBS Records, 1973
George Cukor (Director)

04

OCT

Hurra Die Die Rattles Kommen
The Rattles
Star-Club Records, 1965
Alexander Welbat (Director)

05

OCT

† Oct 6th, 1985 as Nelson Smock Riddle Jr.
in Los Angeles, California, USA

The Great Gatsby
Nelson Riddle
Paramount Records, 1974
Francis Ford Coppola (Director)

06

OCT

* Oct 7th, 1968 as Thomas Edward Yorke
in Wellingborough, UK

Suspiria
Thom Yorke
XL Recordings, 2018
Luca Guadagnino (Director)
Stanley Donwood, Doktor Tchok, Agnes F. (Design)

07

OCT

The Man From U.N.C.L.E
Hugo Montenegro
RCA Records, 1966
Sam Rolfe (Director)

08

OCT

Fanny Hill
Oven Feat. Frank Thomas
Canyon Records, 1969
Russ Meyer (Director)

09

OCT

† Oct 10th,1985 as Yuliy Borisovich Briner in NYC, USA

Taras Bulba
Franz Waxman
United Artists Records, 1962
Waldo & Karl Tunberg (Director)
Frank C. McCarthy (Design)

Shopping Bag
The Partridge Family
Bell Records, 1972
Bernard Slade (Director)
Beverly Weinstein (Design)

11

OCT

Les Vouleurs De La Nuit
Ennio Morricone
General Music France, 1984
Samuel Fuller (Director)

12

OCT

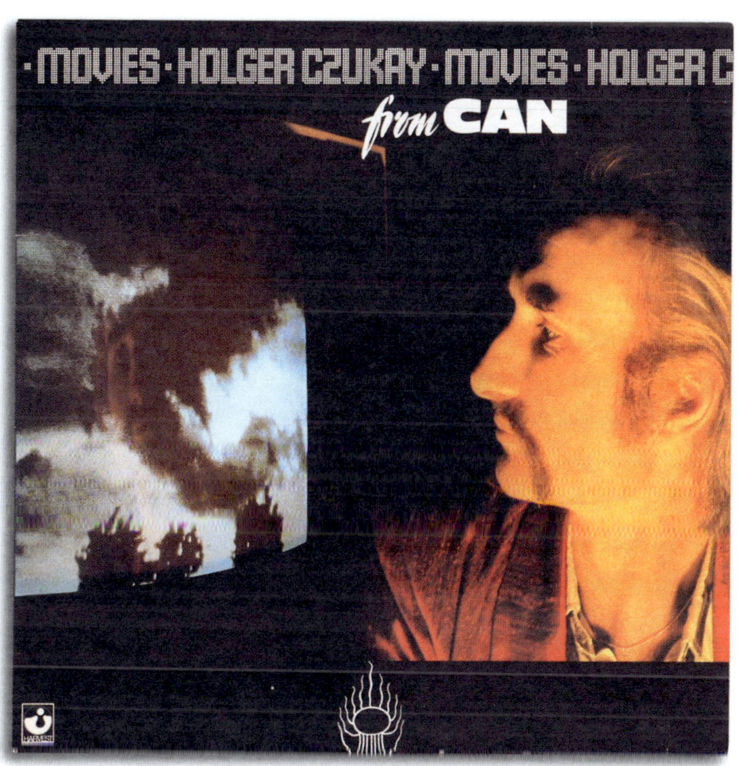

Movies
Holger Czukay
Harvest, 1979
Hermann Schulte (Photo)

13

OCT

* Oct 14th, 1927 as Sir Roger George Moore
in Stockwell, London, UK

007 Live And Let Die
George Martin
United Artists Records, 1973
Guy Hamilton (Director)

14

OCT

Dueling Banjos Deliverance
Eric Weissberg And Steve Mandell
Warner Bros. Records, 1973
John Boorman (Director)

15

OCT

† Oct 16th, 1990 as Arthur William Blakey
in New York City, USA

Les Liaisons Dangereuses
Art Blakey's Jazz Messengers
Epic Records, 1962
Roger Vadim (Director)
Mozelle Thompson (Design)

16 OCT

Thank God It's Friday
Various Artists
Casablanca Records, 1978
Robert Klane (Director)

17

OCT

Perry Rhodan – SOS Aus Dem Weltall
Antón García Abril, Marcello Giombini
Diggler Records, 2003
Primo Zeglio (Director)
Thomas Gross (Design)

18

OCT

Peur Sur La Ville
Ennio Morricone
Wewantsounds, 2020
Henri Verneuil (Director)
Eric Adrian Lee (Design)

19

OCT

That Summer!
Various Artists
Arista Records, 1979
Harley Cokliss (Director)
Graphyk (Design)

20

OCT

Chariots Of Fire
Vangelis
Polydor Records, 1981
Hugh Hudson (Director)
Alwyn Clayden (Design)

21

OCT

† Oct 22nd, 1987 as Lino Ventura in Saint-Cloud, France

Der Maulwurf
Ennio Morricone
General Music France, 1983
Yves Boisset (Director)

Pele
Sergio Mendes
Atlantic Records, 1977
François Reichenbach (Director)

Ascenseur Pour L'Échafaud
Miles Davis
Jazz Wax Records, 1957
Louis Malle (Director)

24

OCT

Together Brothers
Barry White
PYE Records, 1974
Jack L. Levy (Design)
William A. Graham (Director)

25

OCT

Blue Hawaii
Elvis Presley
RCA Victor, 1961
Norman Taurog (Director)

26

OCT

Jubilee X
Various Artists
E.G. Records Ltd., 1978
Derek Jarman (Director)

27

OCT

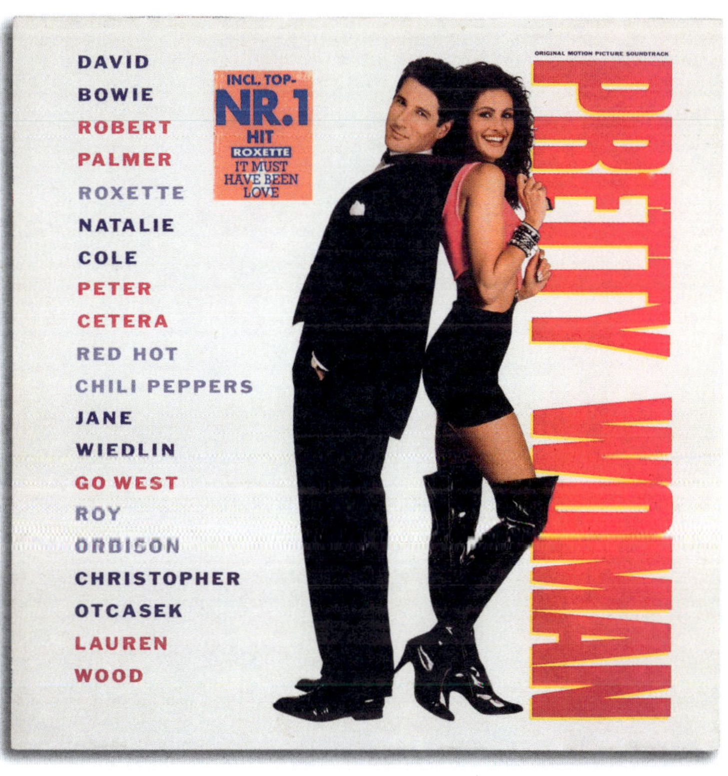

* Oct 28th, 1967 as Julia Fiona Roberts in Atlanta, Georgia, USA

Pretty Woman
Various Artists
EMI Records Ltd., 1990
Garry Marshall (Director)

28

OCT

Zwei Asse Trumpfen Auf
The Fantastic Oceans
Ariola, 1981
Sergio Corbucci (Director)

29

OCT

Silent Running
Peter Schickele
Decca, 1972
Douglas Trumbull (Director)
George Akimoto (Illustration)

30

OCT

Halloween

It's The Great Pumpkin, Charlie Brown
Vince Guaraldi
Craft Recordings, 2018
Charles M. Schulz (Director)
Carrie Smith (Design)

31

OCT

Valley Of The Dolls
Dory Previn And Andre Previn
20th Century Fox Records, 1967
Mark Robson (Director)

01

NOV

Original Filmsoundtrack

DAS LETZTE EINHORN

»THE LAST UNICORN«

Composed and arranged by

JIMMY WEBB

Performed by

AMERICA

Das Letzte Einhorn – The Last Unicorn
Jim Webb & America
Virgin Records, 1982
Arthur Rankin Jr. (Director)

02

NOV

* Nov 3rd, 1933 as John Barry Prendergast in York, UK

Black Hole
John Barry
Buena Vista Records, 1979
Gary Nelson (Director)

03

NOV

Die Kette
Dieter Reith & Tender Aggression
ShowUp Records, 2014
Rolf Von Sydow (Director)
Roland Junker (Design)

04

NOV

* Mar 7th, 1984 in Baltimore, Maryland, USA

Alex Somers
Music From The Film Captain Fantastic
Lakeshore Records, 2016
Ingibjörg Birgisdottir (Design)

05

NOV

Russ Meyer's Lorna, Vixen, Faster Pussycat! Kill! Kill!
Various Artists
Normal Rec., 1995
Russ Meyer (Director)
Thomas Hartlage (Design)

06

NOV

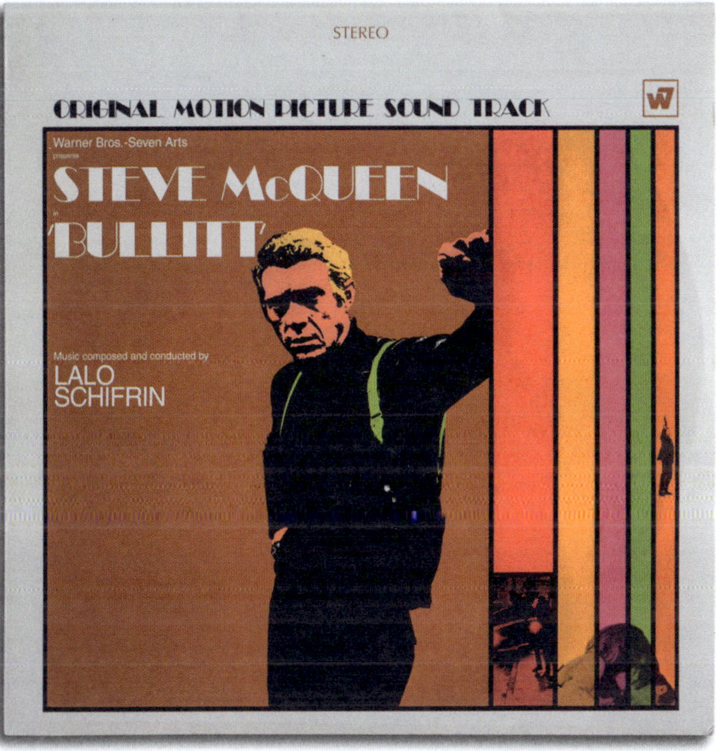

| Nov 7th, 1980 as Steven Terrence "Steve" McQueen
in Ciudad Juarez, Mexico

Bullitt
Lalo Schifrin
Warner Bros. Records, 1968
Peter Yates (Director)
Ed Trasher (Design)

07

NOV

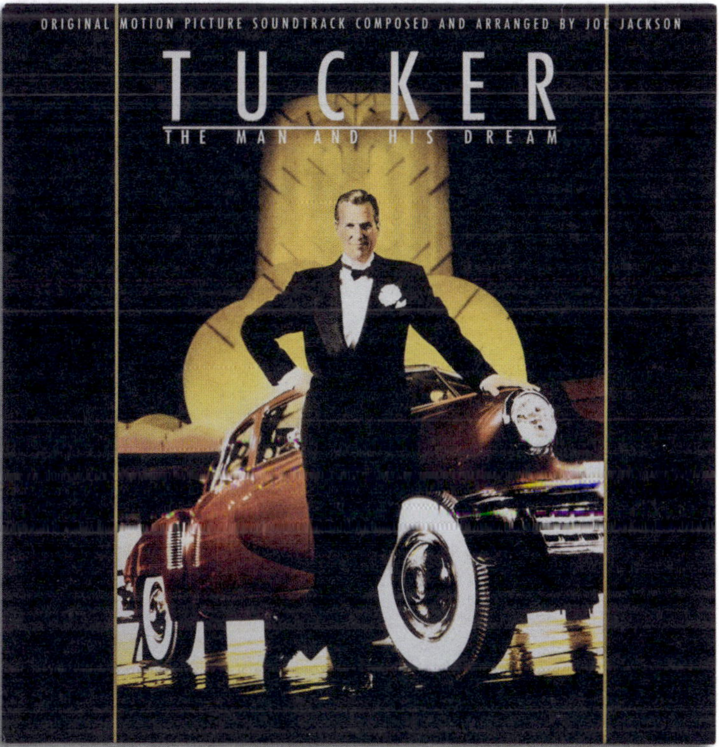

ORIGINAL MOTION PICTURE SOUNDTRACK COMPOSED AND ARRANGED BY JOE JACKSON

TUCKER

THE MAN AND HIS DREAM

Tucker- The Man And His Dream
Joe Jackson
A&M Records, 1988
Francis Ford Coppola (Director)

08

NOV

Let's Make Love – The Latest Blonde
Marilyn Monroe
All Round Trading, 1986
George Cukor (Director)

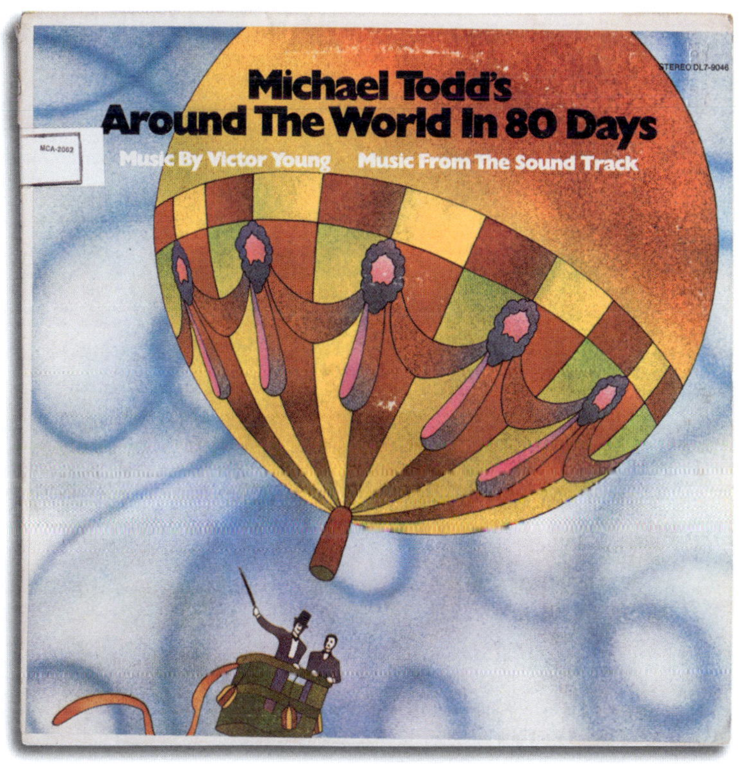

Around The World In 80 Days
Victor Young
Decca Records, 1957
John Farrow, Michael Anderson (Director)
James Sullivan (Design)

10

NOV

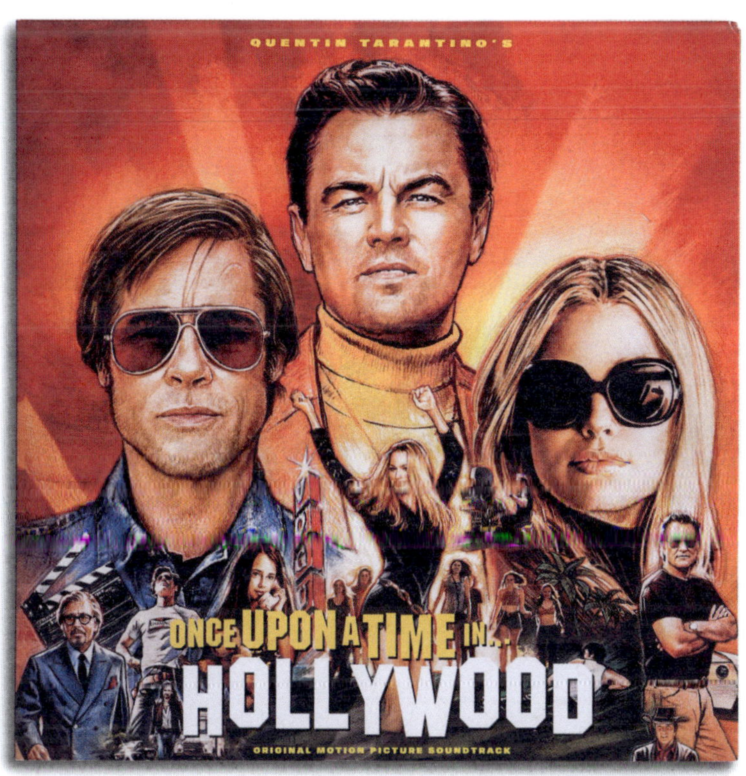

* Nov 11th, 1974 as Leonardo Wilhelm "Leo" Di Caprio in Los Angeles, California, USA

Once Upon A Time In Hollywood
Various Artists
Columbia Records, 2019
Quentin Tarantino (Director)

11

NOV

* Nov 12th, 1945 as Neil Percival Young in Toronto, Canada

Dead Man
Neil Young
Vapor Records, 1996
Jim Jarmusch (Director)
Gary Burden (Design)

12

NOV

Live For Life
Francis Lai
United Artists Records, 1967
Claude Lelouch (Director)

13

NOV

New-York 1997
Various Artists
Milan Records, 1981
John Carpenter (Director)
Joe Alves (Design)

14

NOV

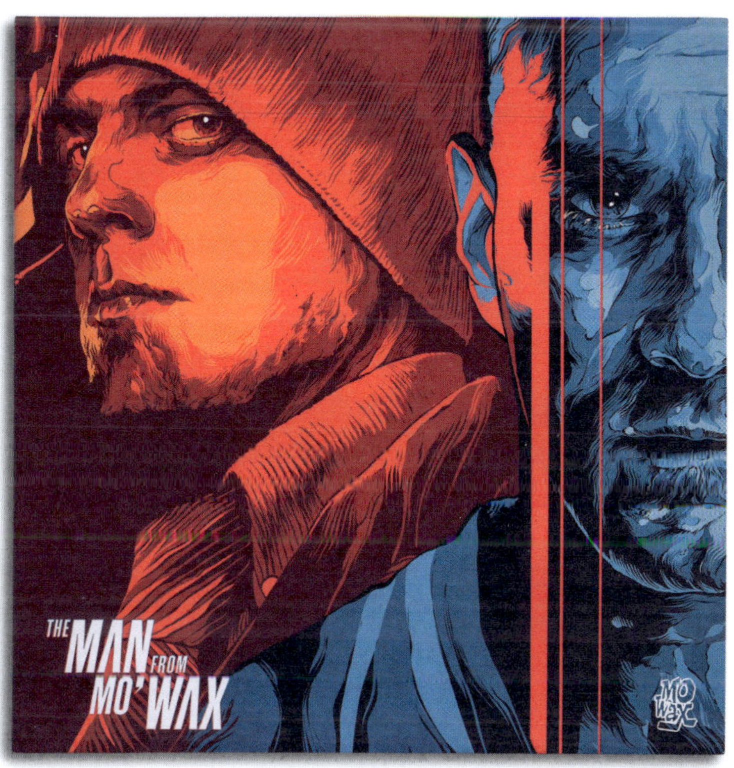

The Man From Mo' Wax
Various Artists
Universal Records, 2018
Matthew Jones (Director)

15

NOV

† Nov 16th, 1960 as William Clark Gable
in Los Angeles, California, USA

Gone With The Wind
Max Steiner
MGM Records, 1967
Victor Fleming (Director)

16

NOV

Filmmusik
Irmin Schmidt
Spoon Records, 1980
Hark Bohm, Reinhard Hauff, Alexander von Eschwege (Director)

17

NOV

All This And World War II
Lennon & McCartney
Warner Records, 1976
Tony Palmer (Director)
Clyde Terry & Jack Room (Design)

18

NOV

Psycho II
Jerry Goldsmith
MCA Records, 1983
Richard Franklin (Director)

19

NOV

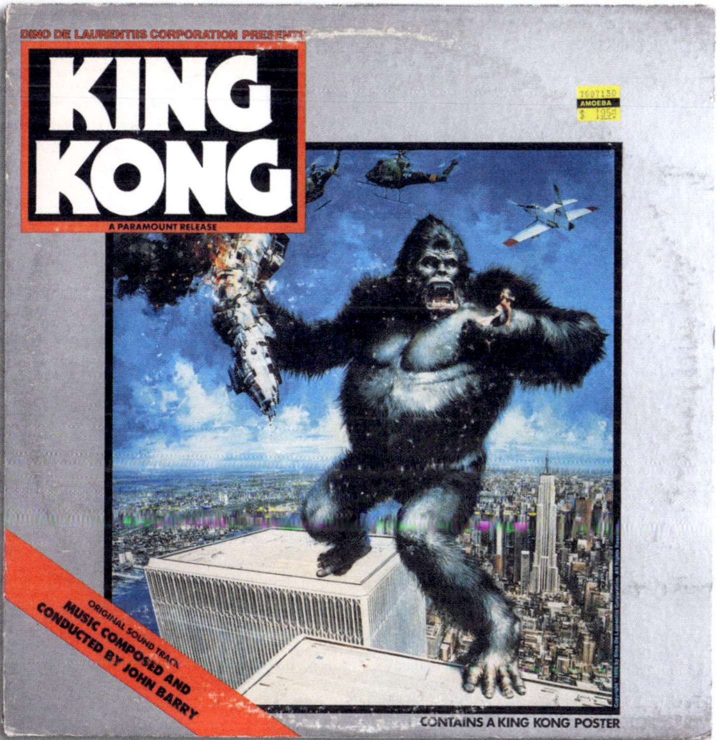

King Kong
John Barry
Reprise Records, 1976
John Guillermin (Director)

Uhrwerk Orange
Various Artists
Warner Bros. Records, 1972
Stanley Kubrick (Director)
Philip Castle (Design)

21

NOV

O Brother, Where Art Thou?
Various Artists
Lost Highway, 2004
Joel & Ethan Coen (Director)

22

NOV

† Nov 23rd, 1991 as Klaus Kinski in Lagunitas, California, USA

Codename Wildgeese
Eloy
Milan Records, 1984
Antonio Margheriti (Director)

23

NOV

* Nov 24th, 1954 as Emir Kusturica
in Sarajevo, Former Yugoslavia

Arizona Dream
Goran Bregovic
Mercury Records, 2018
Emir Kusturica (Director)

24

NOV

† Nov 25th, 2016 as David Hamilton in Paris, France

Bilitis
Francis Lai
Editions 23, 1977
David Hamilton (Director)
David Hamilton (Design)

25

NOV

Original Motion Picture Score
Music Composed by Gato Barbieri

An ALBERTO GRIMALDI Production

Marlon Brando

Last Tango in Paris

UA

† Nov 26th, 2018 as Bernardo Bertolucci in Rome, Italia

Last Tango In Paris
Gato Barbieri
United Artists Records, 1973
Bernardo Bertolucci (Director)

26

NOV

* Nov 27th, 1940 as Bruce Lee as Lee-Jun-Fan
in San Francisco, California, USA

The Big Boss
Joseph Koo / Wang Fu Ling*
Tam, 1971
Masashi Akiyama (Director)

DAGORED

STEREO red106

ORIGINAL MOTION PICTURE SOUNDTRACK

COMPOSED and DIRECTED by ENNIO MORRICONE

LE FOTO PROIBITE DI UNA SIGNORA PER BENE

NOV 10TH, 1928 as Ennio Morricone in Rome, Italy

Le Foto Probite Di Una Signora Per Bene
Ennio Morricone
Dagored, 1999
Luciano Ercoli (Director)

28

NOV

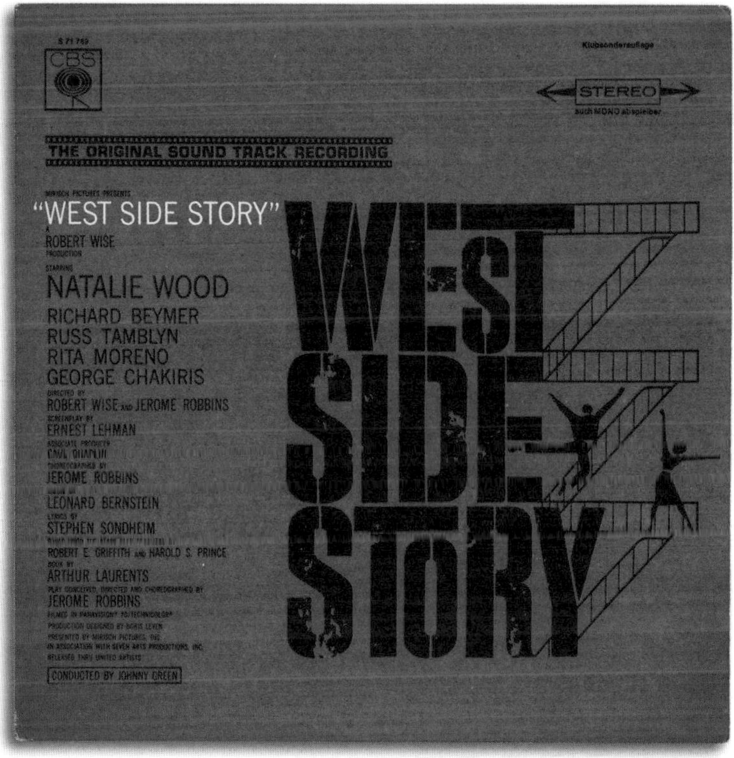

† Nov 29th, 1981 as Natalie Wood
on Santa Catalina Island, California, USA

West Side Story
Leonard Bernstein
CBS Records, 1961
Robert Wise & Jerome Robbins (Director)

29

NOV

Can't Stop The Music
Village Music, David London, Ritchie Family
Metronome, 1980
Nancy Walker (Director)

30

NOV

CBS 73875

MUSIC FROM THE WOODY ALLEN FILM
INCLUDING SELECTIONS FROM THE ORIGINAL SOUNDTRACK

MANHATTAN

MUSIC BY GEORGE GERSHWIN

NEW YORK PHILHARMONIC
CONDUCTED BY ZUBIN MEHTA
GARY GRAFFMAN, PIANO

* Dec 1st, 1935 as Heywood Woody Allen in Bronx, NYC

Manhattan
George Gershwin
CBS Records, 1979
Woody Allen (Director)

01

DEC

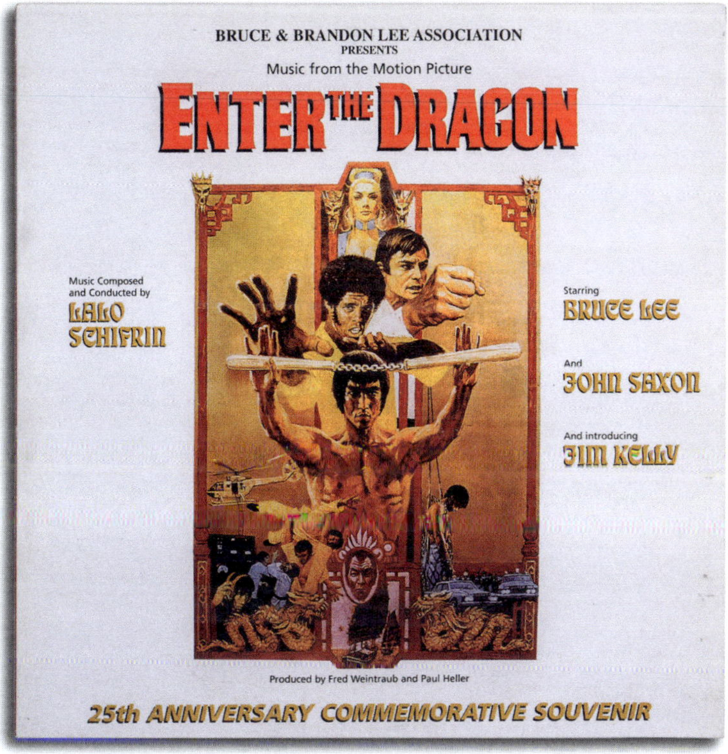

BRUCE & BRANDON LEE ASSOCIATION
PRESENTS
Music from the Motion Picture
ENTER THE DRAGON

Music Composed and Conducted by
LALO SCHIFRIN

Starring
BRUCE LEE
And
JOHN SAXON
And introducing
JIM KELLY

Produced by Fred Weintraub and Paul Heller

25th ANNIVERSARY COMMEMORATIVE SOUVENIR

Enter The Dragon
Lalo Schifrin
Warner Bros. Records, 1973
Robert Clouse (Director)
Bob Peak (Design)

02

DEC

RCA
STEREO
NL 33204

CINEMATRE
PRESENTA

Le grandi colonne sonore dei film di ieri, di oggi, di domani.

COLONNA SONORA ORIGINALE DEL FILM

LA DOLCE VITA

E ALTRI CELEBRI FILM DI FELLINI

LA STRADA / LO SCEICCO BIANCO / I VITELLONI
IL BIDONE / LE NOTTI DI CABIRIA
BOCCACCIO 70 / GIULIETTA DEGLI SPIRITI

MUSICHE DI NINO ROTA

Squarci di vita italiana attraverso la fantasia di un grande regista

La Dolce Vita
Nino Rota
RCA Records, 1978
Federico Fellini (Director)

03

DEC

SOUNDTRACK FROM THE
BANNED SOUTH AFRICAN MOVIE

Glenda

SNAKE DANCER 1976

Sonorama

THE HUSTLER · OPUS AFRICA
SHOW ME WHAT YOU ARE
GET IT ON WITH MUSIC
HILLBROW BY NIGHT
THE CLUB · GLENDA
AND OTHERS

STEREO

MUSIC BY ZANE CRONJE & CHARLES SEGAL – VARIOUS ARTISTS

Glenda Snake Dancer
Zane Cronje & Charles Segal
Sonorama Records, 1976
Patrick Haase (Director)

04

DEC

Shaft In Africa
Johnny Pate
ABC Records, 1973
John Guillermin (Director)

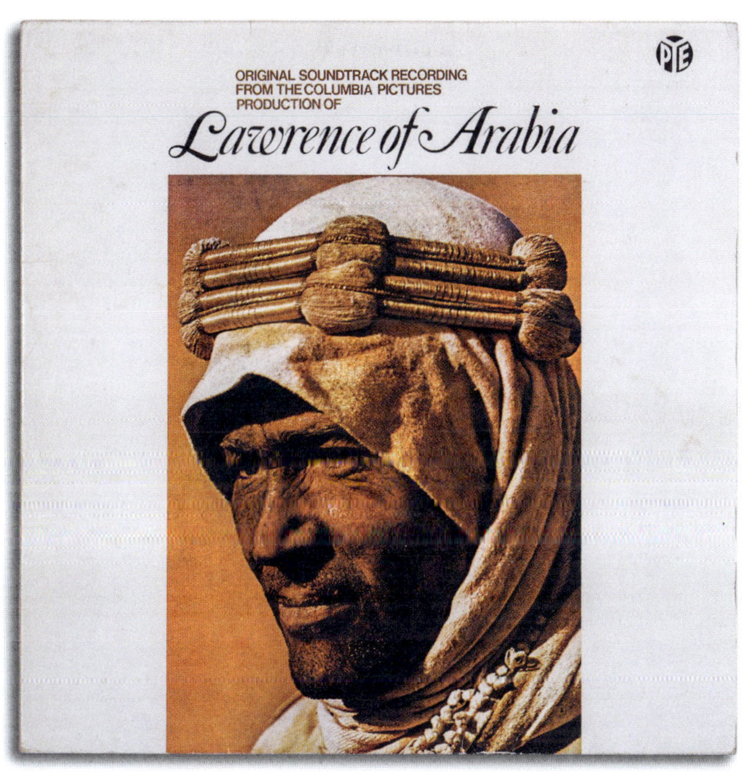

Lawrence Of Arabia
Maurice Jarre, The London Philharmonic Orchestra
Pye Golden Guinea Records, 1967
David Lean (Director)

06

DEC

Love Story
Francis Lai
MCA Records, 1970
Arthur Miller (Director)

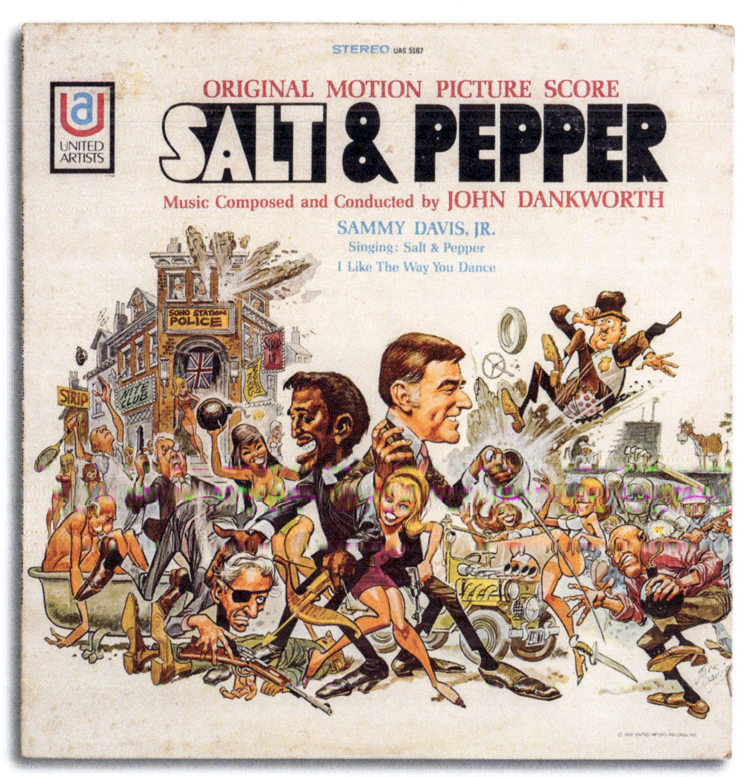

Salt & Pepper
John Dankworth
United Artists Records, 1967
Richard Donner (Director)
Jack Davis (Design)

Vigilante! (Roy Budd Cult Film Soundtracks 1971-1977)
Roy Budd
Discotheque, 2004
Director Unknown
Cover Artists Unknown

09

DEC

Let's Do It Again
Curtis Mayfield
Curtom Records, 1975
Sidney Potier (Director)
Sandy Kossin (Design)

10

DEC

ORIGINAL MOTION PICTURE SOUNDTRACK

POLTERGEIST

STEREO 2315 439

MGM

Poltergeist
Jerry Goldsmith
MGM Records, 1982
Steven Spielberg (Director)

11

DEC

* Dec 12th, 1915 as Francis Albert "Frank" Sinatra
in Hoboken, New Jersey, USA

Pal Joey
Frank Sinatra
Capitol Records, 1957
George Sidney (Director)
Maurice Thomas (Design)

12

DEC

The Hateful Eight
Ennio Morricone
Decca Records, 2015
Quentin Tarantino (Director)

13

DEC

Rubare Alla Mafia E' Un Suicidio
Bobby Womack
Dagored, 2000
Barry Shear (Director)

14

DEC

"Rock All Night" Soundtrack
The Blockbusters, Eddie Beal Combo, Norah Hayes, The Platters
Bear Family Productions Ltd., 1957
Roger Corman (Director)
Roderick Laing (Illustration)

15

DEC

Invito Al Viaggio
Nina Scott
Delta, 1983
Peter Del Monte (Director)

16

DEC

La Cugina
Ennio Morricone
Overdrive, 1974
Aldo Lado (Director)
Solomacello (Design)

17

DEC

* Dec 18th, 1946 as Steven Allan Spielberg
in Cincinnati, Ohio, USA

E.T. The Extra-Terrestrial
John Williams
MCA Records, 1982
Steven Spielberg (Director)

18

DEC

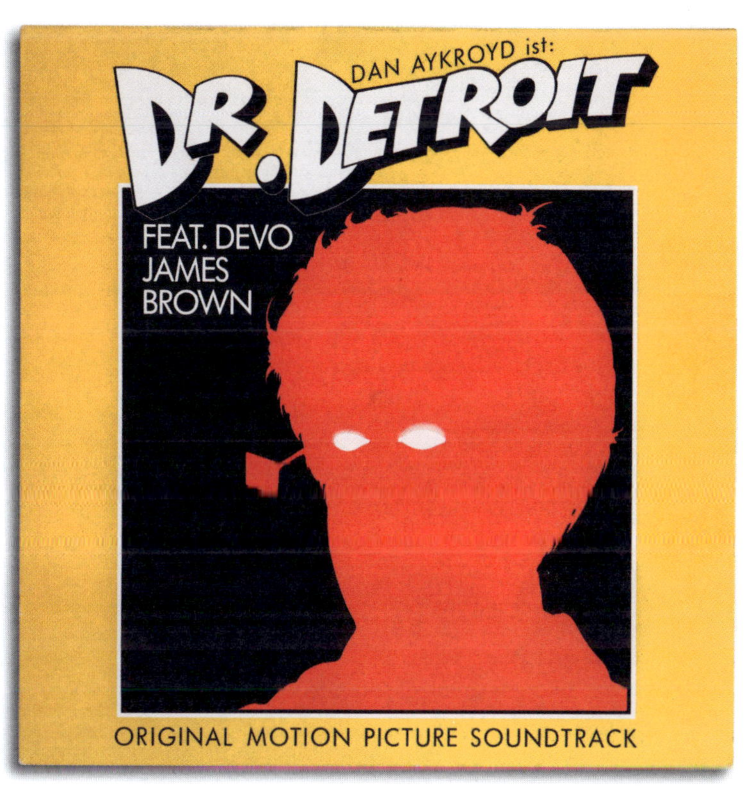

Dr. Detroit
Various Artists
WEA, 1984
Michael Pressman (Director)

Billie
Dominic Frontiere
United Artists Records, 1963
Ronald Alexander (Director)

DYNOVOICE
STEREO
DY 31908

PARAMOUNT PICTURES PRESENTS IN A DINO DE LAURENTIIS PRODUCTION

JANE FONDA
AS
BARBARELLA

PRODUCED BY: Dino De Laurentiis
DIRECTED BY: Roger Vadim
LYRICS AND MUSIC BY: Bob Crewe and Charles Fox
PERFORMED BY: The Bob Crewe Generation Orchestra
SONGS SUNG BY: The Glitterhouse and Bob Crewe

* Dec 21st, 1937 as Jane Seymour Fonda in NYC, USA

Barbarella
Bob Crewe Generation Orchestra
Dynovoice Records, 1968
Roger Vadim (Director)
Bob Mcginnis (Design)

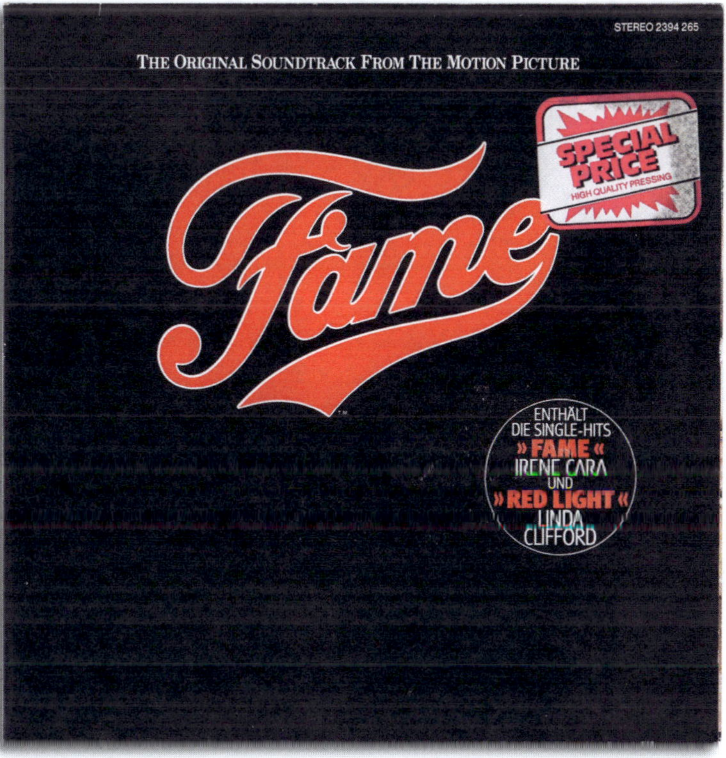

Fame
Various Artists
MGM Records, 1980
Alan Parker (Director)

22

DEC

Zwei Wahnsinnig Starke Typen – Stir Crazy
Tom Scott
RCA Records, 1981
Sidney Poitier (Director)

23

DEC

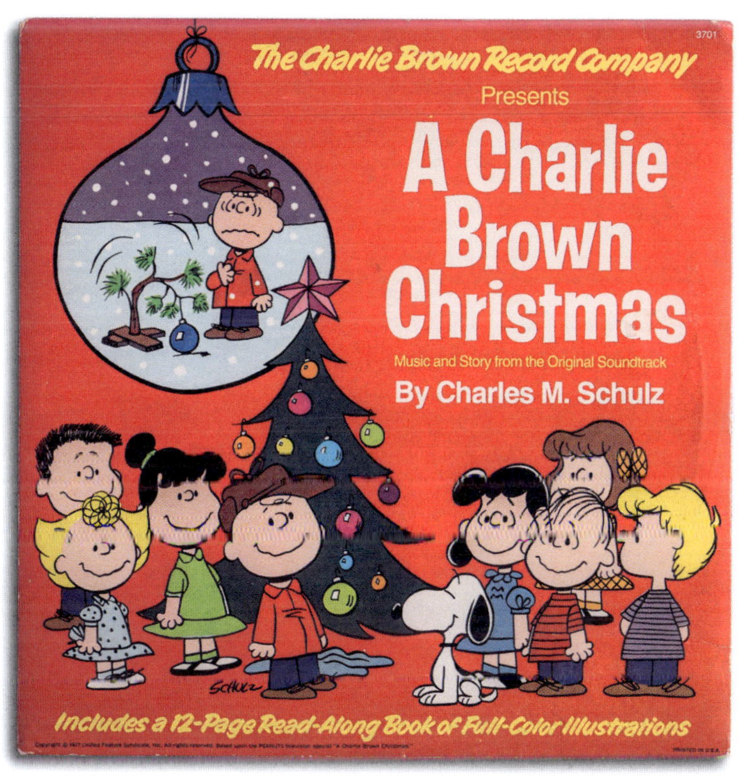

A Charlie Brown Christmas
Charles M. Schulz
Buena Vista Records, 1977
Bill Meléndez (Director)
Charles M. Schulz (Design)

24

DEC

Jesus Of Nazareth
Maurice Jarre
PYE International Records, 1977
Franco Zeffirelli (Director)
Paul Chave (Design)

25

DEC

† Dec 26th, 1999 as Curtis Lee Mayfield in Roswell, Georgia, USA

Let's Do it Again
The Staple Singers & Curtis Mayfield
Curtom Records, 1975
Sidney Poitier (Director)
Sandy Korsin (Illustration)

26

DEC

Rocky IV
Various Artists
Scotti Brothers, 1985
Sylvester Stallone (Director)

27

DEC

"10"
Henry Mancini
Warner Brothers Records, 1979
Blake Edwards (Director)

The Mad, Mad World Of Soundtracks Vol. 2
Various Artists
Universal Jazz, 2001
Stefan Kassel & Matthias Künnecke (Design)

29

DEC

Blow Up
Herbie Hancock
MGM Records, 1966
Michelangelo Antonioni (Director)
Acy R. Lehman (Design)

30

DEC

Reservoir Dogs
Various Artists
MCA Soundtracks, 1992
Quentin Tarantino (Director)
Linda R. Chen (Design)

31

DEC

Imprint

THE ART OF SOUNDTRACK COVERS

Seltmann Publishers
Berlin, Germany
www.seltmannpublishers.com
info@seltmannpublishers.de

Editor: Oliver Seltmann
oliver@seltmann.de

Cover Selection & Backround Research:
Bernd Jonkmanns

Thanks to Dieter Braun, Paul Rechlin, Holger Rohmig, Ingo Scheel and the Recordstore Plattenrille, Hamburg for providing their record collection.

Art Direction: Sandro Heindel, Stefan Küstner

Print Production by Seltmann Printart

This project is an homage to the great and glorious decade of vinyl records and their wonderfully designed covers. With this project, we aim to showcase and preserve the covers as well as their high level of artistic power and profound meaningfulness. Every cover has been selected from personal vinyl collections and individually photographed. We thank everyone involved for their unique artistic work that made this project possible. If you have any questions or suggestions, please do not hesitate to contact us personally.

ISBN 978-3-949070-05-1